STAR TREK THE NEXT GENERATION®
BEGINNINGS

MIKE **CARLIN**
WRITER

PABLO **MARCOS**
PENCILLER

CARLOS **GARZON**
ARNE **STARR**
INKERS

CARL **GAFFORD**
COLORIST

BOB **PINAHA**
LETTERER

BASED ON **STAR TR**
CREA

D1424726

JENETTE KAHN
PRESIDENT & EDITOR-IN-CHIEF

PAUL LEVITZ
EXECUTIVE VICE PRESIDENT &
PUBLISHER

ROBERT GREENBERGER
EDITOR, ORIGINAL SERIES

BOB KAHAN
EDITOR, COLLECTED EDITION

ROBBIN BROSTERMAN
ART DIRECTOR

JOE ORLANDO
VP-CREATIVE DIRECTOR

BRUCE BRISTOW
VP-SALES & MARKETING

PATRICK CALDON
VP-FINANCE & OPERATIONS

TERRI CUNNINGHAM
MANAGING EDITOR

CHANTAL D'AULNIS
VP-BUSINESS AFFAIRS

LILLIAN LASERSON
VP & GENERAL COUNSEL

SEYMOUR MILES
VP-ASSOCIATE PUBLISHER

BOB ROZAKIS
EXECUTIVE DIRECTOR-PRODUCTION

STAR TREK: THE NEXT GENERATION -
BEGINNINGS ISBN 1 85286 643 8
First edition: August 1995. STAR TREK:
THE NEXT GENERATION is a trademark
of Paramount Pictures. Published by
Titan Books Ltd, 42-44 Dolben Street,
London SE1 0UP, by arrangement with
DC Comics under exclusive licence from
Paramount Pictures, the trademark
owner. Copyright © 1995 Paramount
Pictures. All Rights Reserved.
Originally published in single magazine
form as STAR TREK: THE NEXT
GENERATION 1-6. Copyright © 1988
Paramount Pictures. All Rights
Reserved. The stories, characters, and
incidents featured in this publication
are entirely fictional.
Cover painting by Bill Sienkiewicz.

Printed in Canada.
10 9 8 7 6 5 4 3 2 1

IT WAS A SUMMER AFTERNOON IN 1987. I WAS UP IN THE ART DEPARTMENT AT PARAMOUNT, WORKING FEVERISHLY ON SOMETHING FOR AN EARLY EPISODE OF STAR TREK: THE NEXT GENERATION.

Bob Justman, one of our producers, walked into the office. He was obviously busy with the million-and-one things that always seem to occupy a producer, but he took a moment to ask me how things were going. I admitted that I was tired and that I wasn't sure that I could keep up this pace for an entire season. Bob, who is a veteran of the original *Star Trek* series, smiled wistfully and said, "Mike, you should enjoy this. In years to come, you'll look back on this as a very special time in your life."

Well, that "special time" has lasted longer than any of us dared hope. Through it all, I've always tried to keep Bob's words in mind, to try to remember how lucky I am to be one of the people who gets to help bring the magic to life every week.

My work in the early days of *Star Trek: The Next Generation* involved designing the control panels for the new *Enterprise*. I had been brought in as a graphic designer in part because of my background in theater and in low-budget television commercials. I had learned to try the cheapest way to do something first, before trying more expensive alternatives. It was an approach the producers appreciated, but it meant a lot of work.

Now, over seven years later, it's a little hard to remember how crazy things were back in those early months. Twelve-hour days and seven-day work weeks were quite common, and even then there never seemed to be enough time to do everything the show demanded. Making *Star Trek* seemed every bit as much an adventure as the voyages of

the *Starship Enterprise.*

The design and construction of the *Enterprise*-D sets took just a few weeks. We had an amazingly short period of time in which to do it all. For my part, I wanted to lavish care on each control panel, on each button, every readout, and every label. My responsibilities were only a tiny part of the overall production, but after all, this was the return of Gene Roddenberry's creation, and I was determined to help make this new *Star Trek* a worthy successor to the original. But I quickly learned that the television production process put distinct limits on how much time could be put into any single element of the show.

When I watched the first *Star Trek* as a kid, I used to always wonder why they didn't take fifteen minutes more to do this, or why they didn't spend just a few extra bucks to do that. Working on *Star Trek: The Next Generation*, I quickly learned that the show can be an almost infinite series of "fifteen minutes" and "just a few more dollars." No matter how hard or how long you worked, there was always something else. The problem was, of course, that television production has an inherently limited budget and schedule. And it is these budget and schedule limitations that would seem to make *Star Trek* — or any science-fiction television series — impossible to produce.

I remember one afternoon when I'd just finished the last piece of art for the bridge control panels. Rick Sternbach strolled past my desk and showed me an issue of *Aviation Week* magazine. It was an article about the future of aircraft control systems, predicting that "virtual" controls would eventually replace physical panels. I skimmed the article then turned to Rick and said, "You realize this makes everything I've just done obsolete." Rick grinned, but we both realized that there was neither the time nor the money to redo the bridge instrumentation. Fortunately, no one has complained yet. (In fact, someone from Northrop told me that some of the secret test software for the B-2 stealth bomber was modeled on the *Enterprise*-D bridge instrumentation!)

Are you familiar with the sport of skeet shooting? You shoot at disk-shaped "clay pigeons" that are flung into the air. It's a game of concentration and skill. You have to aim at the target, following it as it flies through the air. You learn to aim a little ahead of the target, so that you're shooting at the point in space where the target will be when your shot reaches it.

What does this have to do with television production? Think of every production decision as a clay pigeon. What color should this be? How much space do you need for this control panel? What does the alien logo look like? How are we going to animate this computer readout? As long as they're launched one at a time, it's not

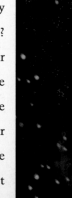

that hard to shoot accurately enough to hit most of the targets. Now imagine that they're being launched several at a time, so that instead of firing at only one target, you have ten. Or fifty. If you take the time to take proper aim, you'll get one, but the other forty-nine will whiz by. You have to point and shoot, point and shoot, point and shoot. If you're good, you'll get at least a few. If you're really good, you'll get more than half. Don't even think about getting all of them unless you want to make yourself crazy. We all got good at pointing and shooting.

As time passed, we all climbed the *Star Trek* learning curve. There was no way to work much harder or longer, but we did learn to work more effectively, to get a lot more "bang" for our production dollars. As has been noted elsewhere, one of the greatest special effects we achieve on a weekly basis is the illusion that we spend a lot more money than we really do.

The results of our learning experiences are pretty clear if you look at our early episodes and compare them to the work we did toward the end of the series. Things that were very difficult for us during the first season became (relatively) easy later on. I remember doing the graphics for the *U.S.S. Stargazer* bridge for "The Battle." It took nearly two solid weeks of 12-plus-hour days, seven days a week. Seven years later, the bridge of the *Starship Pasteur* for "All Good Things" seemed almost easy,

even though it was a more complicated set. Multiply this learning effect by every department on the show, and you'll get an idea of how far we all have come.

It has been said that our *Star Trek* television production teams each produce the equivalent of half a motion picture every week. This is no minor achievement. Look at it this way: The *Star Trek* feature films (which are themselves very tightly budgeted compared to many other major science-fiction movies) usually have about sixteen weeks of prep time before production, then about ten weeks of actual shooting to produce two hours of finished film. By contrast, the television versions of *Star Trek* normally have about seven working days of preparation for a typical episode, followed by seven or eight days of actual shooting to produce an hour's worth of film.

Star Trek is not unique in this respect. Similar (and often more severe) constraints apply to every other television show on the air. When my friends ask me about other science-fiction shows, they will somehow assume that I must somehow dislike them. After all, they're the enemy, right? Wrong! As much as I like *Star Trek*, I love watching a show when I have absolutely no idea what's going to happen. (My wife, Denise, and I both count ourselves among the legion of *Babylon 5* fans!) I love it when all the surprises are fresh, and when someone *else* had to sweat the details. And it is

precisely for this reason that I'm fond of the comic book adventures of the *Starship Enterprise*.

After all, not only can they tell stories that I can be completely surprised by, but because of the nature of the medium, they don't have to be worried about pesky budgetary constraints. They can show fleets of alien starships without worrying about visual effects budgets, and they can make planet exteriors as big as they want without worrying about how much they can squeeze into stage 16. (Richard James, our production designer, would be incredibly envious.)

When I first learned that DC Comics was going to do a series based on *Star Trek: The Next Generation*, I was pretty excited. After all, if they did the book, they would have to show the ship. When they showed the ship, they would have to show the ship's interiors. When they showed the interiors, they would have to show the control panels. My stuff.

Naturally, I wanted my control panels to be shown off in full glorious detail, so I immediately made photocopies of all the panel layouts and sent them to DC. I sent them copies of the set blueprints. I sent them copies of memos. Technical manuals. Diagrams. Just about anything that Paramount's licensing department would let me send them. (Later on, I even took several rolls of photos of the *Enterprise*-D model and the interior sets for reference by DC's artists.)

When the first issue (reprinted here!) came out, I immediately rushed out and bought four copies. After all, not only did they use my stuff, but Bill Sienkiewicz used it on the cover! Okay, maybe these early issues left some room for improvement, but it is somehow appropriate that this closely parallels *Star Trek*'s early episodes.

As I write this, the first episode of *Star Trek: Voyager* has just premiered on the United Paramount Network. It is yet another beginning for *Star Trek*, yet another chance to climb the learning curve to do what we hope will be even more wonderful adventures among the cosmos. As proud as I am of what we accomplished seven years ago in launching the *Enterprise*-D, I am even more excited by this fresh start, which may well carry Gene Roddenberry's dream into the twenty-first century.

Boldly, where none have gone before.

*Michael Okuda is in charge of graphics on the **Star Trek** TV shows and movies. He is also co-author of the **Star Trek: The Next Generation Technical Manual,** the **Star Trek Encyclopedia** and the **Star Trek Chronology,** all published by Pocket Books.*

G-3379

7

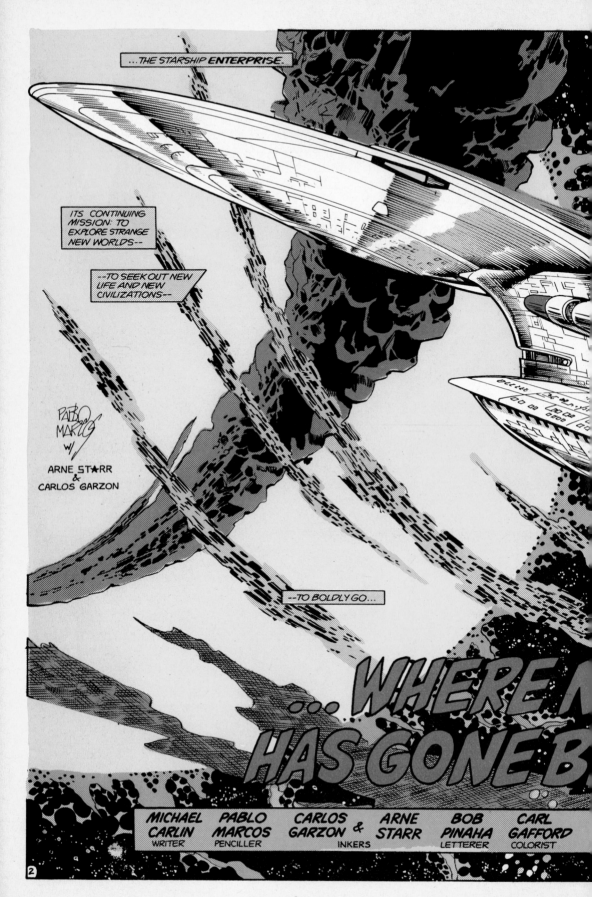

CAPTAIN'S LOG: STARDATE 41187.5

THE U.S.S. ENTERPRISE SLICES THROUGH THE PITCH THICKNESS OF AN UNMAPPED SECTOR LIKE A SHAFT.

HER OWN LEGEND, AND THOSE OF HER PREDECESSORS, SERVING US AS FUEL FOR THIS AND ALL HER SUBSEQUENT MISSIONS.

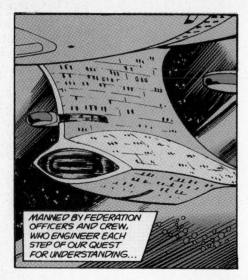

MANNED BY FEDERATION OFFICERS AND CREW, WHO ENGINEER EACH STEP OF OUR QUEST FOR UNDERSTANDING...

...PROPELLING US FURTHER AND DEEPER THAN EVER BEFORE--

--IN A SEEMINGLY ENDLESS THIRST FOR KNOWLEDGE AND HARMONY.

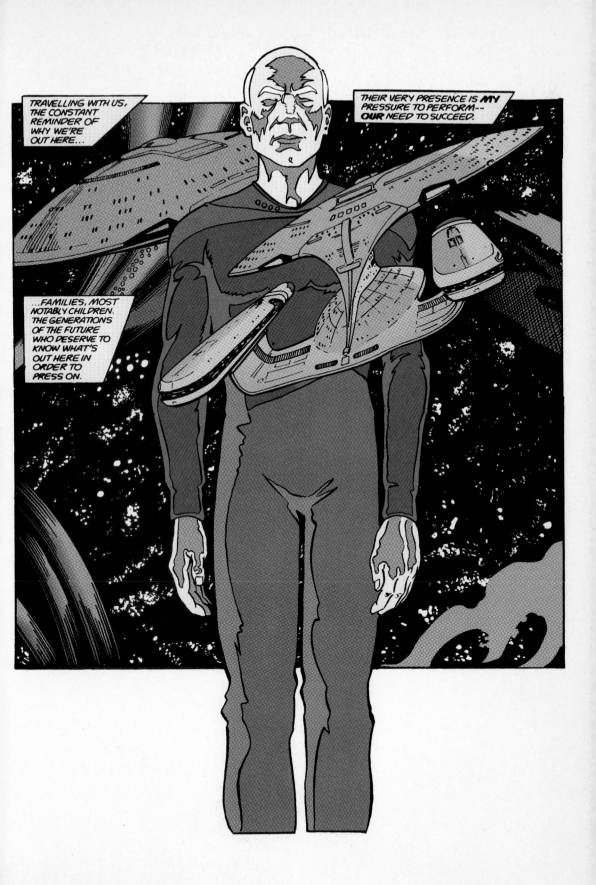

AS A MATTER OF FACT I'VE NEVER TRULY BEEN COMFORTABLE SHARING MY "VISIONS" AS ANY KIND OF GAUGE, SINCE THE MARGIN FOR ERROR IS A DISTINCT REALITY.

EXCUSE THE INTERRUPTION, SIRS... BUT SENSORS INDICATE WE'RE ENTERING THE TRI-BETALINE SYSTEM.

IT'S QUITE A VAST SYSTEM-- IT'LL BE ELEVEN STANDARD MINUTES BEFORE WE CAN MAKE ANY AUDIO OR VISUAL CONTACT WITH T-B 13.

I REALIZE THIS MAY SOUND ODD --BUT I'M VERY EXCITED ABOUT THIS MISSION.

AYE, COMMANDER RIKER...SHE'S ENTERED AND LOGGED.

MUST SAY, SEEING T-B 13 AFTER ALL THIS TRAVELLING TIME'S GOING TO BE A SIGHT FOR SORE EYES.

AWAITING FURTHER ORDERS, SIRS.

YOUR TEA, SIR.

THANK YOU, MISTER RAYMOND.

IT WILL BE MOST INTERESTING OBSERVING ANY FORMS OF LIFE WE MIGHT ENCOUNTER ON T-B 13.

NO FEDERATION VESSEL'S EVER BEEN--

COMFORTABLE, MISTER RIKER?

SORRY, SIR.

AS I WAS SAYING...

STILL A BIT CONSCIOUS OF CAPTAIN PICARD'S REPUTATION-- TRYING TO RELAX...

TRYING A LITTLE TOO HARD!

VISUAL CONTACT WITH T-B 13, SIR.

MAINTAIN, MISTER WORF--

--AND COMMENCE COLLECTING ALL PERTINENT INFORMATION.

OUR SHIP'S COMPUTER CONTAINS ABSOLUTELY NO INFORMATION ON THIS SECTOR.

AYE, SIR...

SHOULDN'T BE ANY PROBLEM.

COMPUTER--

--SCAN T-B I3 AT THESE CO-ORDINATES, AND THEN--

--SHOW ME WHAT YOU HAVE.

HMMM. STUFF LIKE DIAMETER AND CURRENT DISTANCE FROM US...

NOT A WHOLE LOT MORE WE CAN GET AT THIS RANGE, SIR.

WE'RE GOING TO HAVE TO WAIT A SECOND OR TWO FOR ANY MORE INFO.

WE'VE WAITED THIS LONG-- ANOTHER MOMENT SHOULDN'T HURT.

IN THE TIME IT'S TAKEN FOR YOU TO REPORT, MISTER WORF--

--WE'VE PROBABLY COME WITHIN RANGE.

I'M WELL AWARE OF THAT, SIR--

8

--BUT A LITTLE SMALL TALK DOESN'T HURT EITHER.

HANG ON-- WE ARE INDEED IN RANGE NOW.

COMPUTER-- TELL US ABOUT T-B 13.

T-B 13: CARBON BASED--CLASS M PLANET.

SENTIENT HUMANOIDS DOMINANT--UNCLASSIFIED RACE.

MORE IN-DEPTH INPUT NECESSARY FOR FURTHER INFORMATION.

MISTER WORF--ESTABLISH CONTACT WITH THE SENTIENTS, USE ALL KNOWN FREQUE--

CAPTAIN! EXCUSE THE INTERRUPTION-- BUT THIS HAS GONE ON LONG ENOUGH!

I'VE WAITED WEEKS FOR CERTAIN MEDICAL SUPPLIES AND I SIMPLY CANNOT--

DOCTOR CRUSHER-- YOU'RE ABUSING YOUR BRIDGE CLEARANCE...

SIR--?

I'VE ESTABLISHED CONTACT WITH THE PEOPLE OF T-B 13.

THIS IS **NOT** THE TIME OR PLACE FOR THIS DISCUSSION!

AND I'VE TOLD YOU BEFORE ABOUT BRINGING YOUR **SON** UP HERE!

THAT'S IRRELEV--

9

SIR, WE'RE BEING *FIRED* UPON--

--BY SYNTAGUS THELUV!

EVERYONE ALL RIGHT?

I'M OKAY, CAPTAIN PICARD!

WHERE'S THE BOY? WESLEY--?

LT. YAR--MAN YOUR SECURITY POST...

AYE, SIR!

NCC-1701D

SHOULDN'T WE HAVE OUR SHIELDS UP?

LT.-- CHANNEL THE SHIP'S AUXILIARY POWER TO DEFLECTORS!

I'M CHIEF SECURITY OFFICER, KID--

--I *KNOW* HOW TO ACTIVATE THE DEFLECTOR SHIELDS!

DOCTOR, TAKE YOUR SON AND VACATE MY BRIDGE IMMEDIATELY!

WE CANNOT HAVE THE DISTRACTIONS YOU'RE CAUSING WHILE UNDER FIRE!

SORRY, CAPTAIN-- WE'LL GO.

11

MISTER RIKER... PUT THE ALIENS ON HOLD--

--AND JOIN DEANNA AND MYSELF IN MY *READY ROOM*.

AYE, CAPTAIN.

WORF, KEEP THE THELUVIANS ON LINE.

WILL DO, SIR.

THIS *IS* A BIT OF AN AWKWARD POSITION, I'M AFRAID.

AND I WOULD VALUE ANY INPUT EITHER OF YOU MIGHT OFFER.

PERHAPS WE *SHOULD* RE-EVALUATE THE WISDOM OF SENDING AN AWAY TEAM DOWN TO SYNTAGUS THELUV AT THIS PARTICULAR TIME.

WE *ARE* RECEIVING RATHER CONFUSING SIGNALS AS TO THEIR INTENT.

WELL, I THINK AN AWAY TEAM IS THE *ONLY* WAY TO FIND ANYTHING OUT FOR SURE.

BUT THE RISKS MAY BE TOO GREAT--

--I CAN'T SHAKE THE FEELING THAT OUR REMOTE SCANS WILL HAVE TO SUFFICE AS OUR CONTACT WITH SYNTAGUS THELUV FOR THE MOMENT.

THAT'S EXACTLY WHAT I'M ON ABOUT, SIR-- WE CANNOT KNOW ANYTHING ABOUT THE THELUVIANS WITH- OUT *PERSONAL* CONTACT!

POINT WELL TAKEN, WILL--THE ENTERPRISE'S MISSION IS TO ESTABLISH SUCH CONTACT WITH STRANGE, NEW WORLDS--

--AND THE FEDERATION NEVER SAID *THAT* WOULD BE EASY!

AT LEAST LET ME RECOMMEND THAT TASHA BE INCLUDED ON THE TEAM-- JUST AS A PRECAUTION.

VERY WELL, RIKER, SELECT YOUR TEAM--

--INCLUDING LT. YAR AS A SECURITY MEASURE.

AYE, SIR.

GIVE ME FIFTEEN MINUTES.

I'LL SUMMON YOU FOR TEAM DEBRIEFING IN TRANSPORTER ROOM 6, CAPTAIN.

SHOULDN'T BE ANYTHING BUT STANDARD DIPLOMATIC PROCEDURES, IF ALL GOES WELL.

13

LIEUTENANTS LAFORGE, DATA AND YAR--TRANSPORTER ROOM 6-- IN TWELVE MINUTES!

AWAY DUTY-- HOW EXCITING.

EXPECTING ANY TROUBLE, SIR?

THEY HAVE INCLUDED *ME* ON THE TEAM, GEORDI...

YEP-- THAT ANSWERS MY QUESTION, ALL RIGHT.

MISTER RIKER...YOU MIGHT WANT TO CONSIDER ADDING ME TO YOUR TEAM... I THINK I COULD BE QUITE USEFUL IN "READING" THE TRUE MOTIVATION BEHIND THE THELUVIANS' ACTIONS. I *HAVE* PROVEN VERY VALUABLE TO YOU ON PREVIOUS MISSIONS...

DEANNA, I'M AFRAID I CANNOT LET WHAT'S HAPPENED BETWEEN US BEFORE STAND IN THE WAY OF THE SUCCESS OF OUR MEETINGS WITH THE THELUVIANS.

SO, COME ON.

WE'VE ONLY GOT EIGHT MINUTES TO GET TO TRANSPORTER 6.

YOU WILL NOT REGRET THIS DECISION, MISTER RIKER.

MISTER WORF-- ALERT THE ALIENS TO EXPECT OUR LANDING CREW...

AND WARN THEM AGAINST ANY MALICIOUS ACTS-- WE COME IN PEACE...

ALREADY DONE SO, SIR...

AND THEY'VE ASSURED ME THERE WILL BE NO PROBLEM-- THEY WELCOME THE FEDERATION.

14

CON AND OP DUTY UNIT B-- REPORT TO THE BRIDGE.

CON AND OP UNIT B--TO THE BRIDGE IMMEDIATELY.

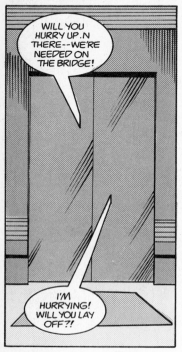

WILL YOU HURRY UP .N THERE--WE'RE NEEDED ON THE BRIDGE!

I'M HURRYING! WILL YOU LAY OFF?!

FORGET IT! I'M NOT GETTING BUSTED BECAUSE YOU'RE TOO BUSY BLOW DRYING YOUR HAIR!

ME? IF YOU DIDN'T TAKE SO LONG IN THERE IN THE FIRST PLACE--

--I'D'VE BEEN READY A LONG TIME AGO!

AAAAAH, TELL IT TO THE REVIEW BOARD!

HOLD THE DOORS FOR ME! HOLD THEM!

IF YOU WOULD JUST HURRY FOR ONCE...

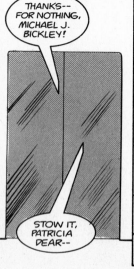

THANKS-- FOR NOTHING, MICHAEL J. BICKLEY!

STOW IT, PATRICIA DEAR--

--UNLESS YOU WANT THE WHOLE BRIDGE TO KNOW OUR PRIVATE AFFAIRS!

BETTER CLAM UP THEN, BIG MOUTH-- 'CAUSE WE'RE HERE!

I KNOW WHERE WE ARE--

15

THIS IS A FEDERATION VESSEL... AND WHILE YOU'RE ABOARD--

CAPTAIN PICARD-- AWAY TEAM IS READY IN TRANSPORTER ROOM 6.

FINE. YOU TWO JUST SIMMER DOWN WHILE I'M GONE...

KEEP HER STEADY...

AND I'LL BE IN TRANSPORTER ROOM 6 IF YOU NEED ME.

AYE, CAPTAIN.

SORRY, CAPTAIN.

DON'T BE SORRY, BICKLEY-- BE CAREFUL!

TAKE ME TO DECK D.

IT USED TO BE MUCH EASIER COMMANDING ONE OF THESE BEAUTIES...

NO KIDS. NO FAMILY SQUABBLES. NO PROBLEMS. AAH, BUT THEY SAY THE DISTANCES WE TRAVERSE...THE TRIPS-- SO LONG...FAMILY UNITS WOULD SIMPLY BE A THING OF THE PAST...

GUESS IT WOULD GET PRETTY TEDIOUS IF ALL I DEALT WITH WERE FEDERATION OFFICER'S DAY IN AND DAY OUT AFTER ALL MY YEARS IN THE FED--

CAPTAIN?!

ARE YOU GOING DOWN TO SYNTAGUS THELUV, SIR?

ARE YOU GOING TO KICK THEIR ALIEN BUTTS FOR ATTACKING US?

EH?

OR ARE YOU GOING TO FOLLOW THE FEDERATION'S PRIME DIRECTIVE AND LAY OFF?

AND THEY STILL HAVEN'T CONVINCED ME THAT THAT WOULD BE THE WORST THING TO HAPPEN TO--

DECK D, SIR.

WESLEY... WHAT CAN I DO FOR YOU?

THEN AGAIN, MAYBE IT **WAS** BETTER HERE THE WAY IT WAS BEFORE.

17

YOUNG MISTER CRUSHER--I MOST CERTAINLY AM *NOT* GOING DOWN TO KICK ANY BUTTS...

...BUT I AM SENDING A TEAM DOWN TO INVESTIGATE THIS PLANET AND ITS INHABITANTS.

SURELY FEDERATION REGULATION 12-MJC ALLOWS FOR SOME SORT OF RETALIATORY ACTION--

--WEREN'T *WE* FIRED UPON?

THEN SHOULDN'T WE BE *LEAVING* THIS PLANET'S ORBIT?

THE REGULATION DOES *ALLOW* FOR RETALIATION-- BUT RECOMMENDS AGAINST IT!

THE AUTHORITIES OF SYNTAGUS THELUV SAY THEY ARE *NOT* RESPONSIBLE.

BUT HOW CAN YOU BE *SURE?*

WESLEY--I'M NOT SURE! *THAT'S* WHY WE'RE INVESTIGATING!

LISTEN, I'D LOVE TO ANSWER ALL YOUR QUESTIONS, BUT I'M TRYING TO *RUN* THIS STARSHIP!

WHAT *WERE* YOU DOING DOWN HERE... LYING IN WAIT FOR ME?

WELL, CAPTAIN--

--YOU CAN'T TAKE THE QUESTIONS BUT YOU CAN SURE DISH THEM OUT.

DOCTOR CRUSHER--!

MOM--?

WESLEY, BACK INTO THE SICK BAY, PLEASE.

BUT, MOM...

NO "BUTS", JUST GO.

18

25

NOW, CAPTAIN, IF YOU HONESTLY DO NOT WANT WESLEY TO BE ABLE TO LOCATE YOU AT ANY GIVEN MOMENT, HAVE THE SHIP KEEP FROM PAGING YOU PUBLICLY.

--ESPECIALLY **YOURS**.

LOOK, YOU CANNOT CHANGE WHAT HAPPENED CONCERNING WESLEY'S FATHER...

WHETHER YOU WERE RESPONSIBLE OR NOT--

AND I STRONGLY SUGGEST YOU STOP USING THE TRANSPORTER NEAR MY SICK BAY-- WESLEY'S ALWAYS AROUND HERE.

BEVERLEY, YOU KNOW I'M NOT COMFORTABLE AROUND CHILDREN--

--I WOULDN'T HAVE CHOSEN TO SERVE ABOARD **YOUR** SHIP, IF I DIDN'T THINK WE **BOTH** COULD HANDLE IT.

I'M TRULY SORRY FOR WHAT HAPPENED THEN, BEVERLEY--

PERHAPS, CAPTAIN--

--AND JUST NOW WITH WESLEY.

PERHAPS WE COULD DISCUSS THIS ALL AT A MORE OPPORTUNE TIME?

--BUT PROBABLY NOT FOR A LONG WHILE.

UM...EXCUSE ME, SIR...

CAPTAIN--?

COMMANDER RIKER--?

ARE YOU HAVING ANY TROUBLE WITH THE CRUSHERS, SIR?

ALL READY HERE IN TRANSPORTER ROOM 6, NUMBER ONE?

UH, **YES,** SIR.

19

GOOD...

AWAY TEAM-- READY FOR BRIEFING?

AYE, SIR.

LT. YAR--AS SECURITY OFFICER, WE ALL HOPE YOUR SPECIAL SKILLS WILL NOT BE NEEDED ON SYNTAGUS THELUV.

YOU ARE ALONG AS A SIMPLE REGULATORY PRECAUTION.

MISTER DATA--YOUR DUTIES ARE TO RECORD IN DETAIL BOTH REGULAR AND IRREGULAR ACTIVITIES DOWN BELOW.

COMMANDER DEANNA TROI-- YOUR ABILITIES AS A TELEPATH ARE OF OBVIOUS VALUE WHEN MEETING NEW LIFE-FORMS.

THE THELUVIANS' TRUE MOTIVES ARE OUR MAIN CONCERN ON THIS MISSION.

GEORDI LAFORGE--YOUR PAST CONTRIBUTIONS TO AWAY MISSIONS MAKE YOU AN ASSET TO ANY TEAM.

ALL WORKING UNDER COMMANDER RIKER'S CONSIDERED GUIDANCE--

--IT IS YOUR RESPONSIBILITY, COMMANDER, TO ESTABLISH POSITIVE CONTACT WITH THE THELUVIANS EVEN THOUGH THEIR ACTIONS ARE MORE THAN QUESTIONABLE AT THIS TIME.

I KNOW YOU WILL MAKE THE FEDERATION AND MYSELF PROUD...

...AND I WISH YOU ALL LUCK.

THANK YOU, SIR.

ENSIGN MOEZER-- ENERGIZE.

ENERGIZING, SIR.

27

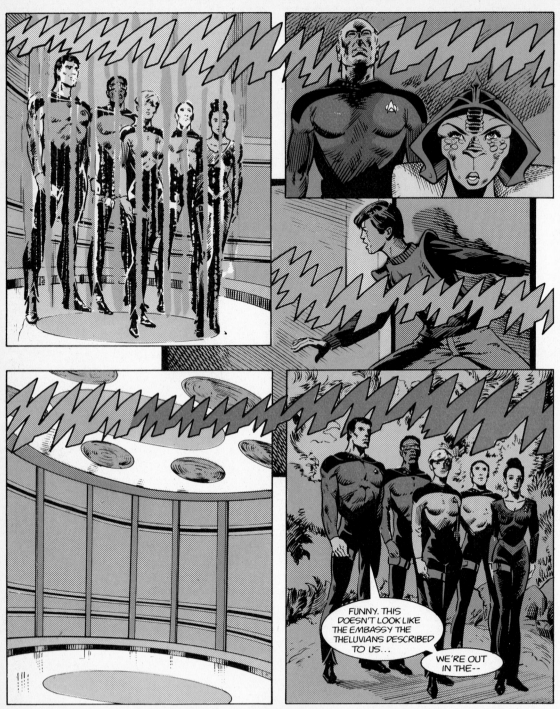

FUNNY. THIS DOESN'T LOOK LIKE THE EMBASSY THE THELUVIANS DESCRIBED TO US...

WE'RE OUT IN THE--

PHASER FIRE!

EVERYONE DOWN!

21

I MIGHT'VE BEEN ABLE TO SENSE THAT ATTACK-- BUT WE HADN'T FULLY MATERIALIZED YET.

NOBODY EXPECTS THE IMPOSSIBLE, DEANNA...

GEORDI... SCAN THE AREA.

OKAY, TASHA...

...YOUR WISH IS MY COMMAND.

NOPE. EVEN WITH MY VISOR--

--THERE'S NOTHING THERE.

AT LEAST NOT DIRECTLY IN FRONT OF--

THAT'S IT, GEORDI-- I'M GETTING SOMETHING...

...TO YOUR LEFT!

THANKS, DEANNA...

YEP...GOT 'EM!

WAIT--THERE'S *LOTS* OF THEM...

...MAYBE *THEY* GOT *US!*

TO OUR LEFT, HUH?

PHASERS AT THE READY.

FIRE AT MY COM--

TASHA, NO!

NOT YET!

22

29

WE CANNOT AFFORD TO MAKE ANY DIPLOMATIC ERRORS IN JUDGMENT...NOT YET!

CAPTAIN PICARD MADE IT CLEAR THAT WE WERE TO STRIVE FOR A POSITIVE FIRST CONTACT.

POSITIVE--? BUT, COMMANDER...

I KNOW IT'S FRUSTRATING, TASHA...BUT THIS IS NOT FEDERATION TERRITORY!

YES, SIR. SORRY, SIR.

I HATE TO SAY THIS, BUT... PHASER FIRE PROBABLY WOULDN'T DO US A WHOLE LOT OF GOOD HERE, NO MATTER WHO GIVES THE ORDERS TO FIRE...

I DON'T LIKE WHAT I'M PICKING UP, NOW--

ALL I CAN TELL YOU IS... IT'S DAMN BIG!

--AND I DON'T EVEN KNOW WHAT I'M REGISTERING!

I'VE NEVER SEEN ANYTHING LIKE IT, SIR.

CAN YOU GIVE ME A MORE DETAILED DESCRIPTION, GEORDI?

I CAN TRY, DATA...IT'S STANDING FIFTY METERS TALL-- WEIGHT ESTIMATED AT THIRTY OR FORTY TONS--

--AND IT'S COVERED WITH SPIKED GUN TURRETS!

HMMM. SOUNDS A LITTLE LIKE A TRIPOLIAN HELLBLAZER-- --THAT'S THE WAR WEAPON EMPLOYED ON TRIPOLI NINE IN THE SECTOR WE JUST CAME FROM. TRUTH TO TELL IT SOUNDS A LITTLE SMALL TO ACTUALLY BE A--

WHATEVER IT IS, WE'RE GOING TO HAVE TO ACT SOON!

DEANNA--ARE YOU PICKING UP SOME KIND OF--

BA DOOOM!

23

30

MISTER WORF--

--ANY WORD FROM BELOW?

CAPTAIN PICARD, GOOD, YOU'RE HERE.

I *HAVE* JUST LOGGED A DISTRESSING MESSAGE...

...THE ALIENS TELL ME THAT THEY ARE *STILL* AWAITING OUR LANDING CREW AT THEIR ROYAL RECEIVING ROOM.

BUT THAT'S NOT POSSIBLE--

--I JUST WATCHED THEM BEAM DOWN!

AND THESE CO-ORDINATES ARE ALL CORRECT.

MISTERS BICKLEY-- SCAN SYNTAGUS THELUV AND *FIND* OUR AWAY CREW!

AYE, SIR.

THIS IS WEIRD! SOMETHING'S BLOCKING MY INSTRUMENTS, CAPTAIN!

JUST LIKE YOU TO GIVE UP SO EASILY...

25

32

I'LL THANK YOU TWO TO SPARE US ALL YOUR DOMESTIC PROBLEMS FOR A CHANGE!

JUST DO SOMETHING ABOUT FINDING MY TEAM!

OR YOU'LL FIND YOURSELVES CONFINED TO YOUR QUARTERS-- *TOGETHER!*

YES, SIR.

SORRY, SIR.

IT'S ALWAYS LIKE THIS WHEN I SEND MY PEOPLE DOWN ALONE--SO FAR FROM THE SHIP.

SOMETIMES I WISH I WAS ALONGSIDE THEM.

I PROBABLY WOULDN'T BE MUCH HELP TO THEM--

--I MIGHT EVEN BE A HINDRANCE... BUT SOMEHOW I'D *FEEL* BETTER.

WHAT COULD POSSIBLY HAVE HAPPENED TO THEM?

IT'S THIS UNCERTAINTY THAT MAKES ME HATE STAYING BEHIND.

MISTER WORF...

YES, SIR?

CONTACT THE THELUVIANS AGAIN, TELL THEM THAT IF ANY HARM BEFALLS OUR CREW-- THERE WILL BE GRAVE TROUBLE BETWEEN THE FEDERATION AND THEIR PEOPLE.

AYE, SIR.

MESSAGE GOING OUT, SIR. ANY- THING ELSE?

THERE IS NOTHING ELSE WE *CAN* DO FOR THE MOMENT.

26

THINGS'VE QUIETED DOWN, EH, DATA?

SO IT WOULD SEEM, GEORDI.

I DON'T TRUST THE QUIET.

NEVER HAVE.

I UNDERSTAND.

I, TOO, WISH THE ATTACK WAS ON AGAIN.

THAT'S NOT EXACTLY WHAT I MEANT, DATA.

DO YOU REALIZE WHAT YOU JUST SAID?

I DO.

IT'S STRANGE-- WHEN THE BOMBS ARE FALLING-- MY ADRENAL FLUID REALLY GETS FLOWING!

AND THERE'S NOTHING LIKE THE THREAT OF TERMINATION TO MAKE YOU REALLY FEEL ALIVE!

SOMETIMES YOU ANDROIDS REALLY THROW ME.

I CAN'T ARGUE THE SENTIMENT-- I JUST WOULDN'T HAVE BEEN ABLE TO PUT IT SO SUCCINCTLY.

BRAAKSSH

GEORDI-- DID YOU HEAR--?

I DID... AND IT WAS A SOUND I TRUST LESS THAN THE QUIET!

UH-OH, AND MY BUILT-IN TRI-CORDER READINGS'RE TELLING ME THAT--

27

THOOOM

CHOOM

--BUT WHERE DO WE RUN *NOW*?

WE'VE RUN OUT OF WOODS AND SMACK INTO A SHEER ROCK WALL!

RUN, DATA! *RUN!*

I AM, GEORDI! I AM--

STILL ENJOYING LIFE TO ITS FULLEST, DATA?

I HOPE SO, BECAUSE THIS LOOKS LIKE THE END!

AT LEAST WE'LL GET A LOOK AT THE CREEPS WHO'VE BEEN STALKING US LIKE WILD GAME!

OH, MY...

VERY SUCCINCT, DATA--AS USUAL.

30

ARTICULATE... AND STRONG, TOO!

JUST PUT HIM OVER HERE, DATA-- LET ME SCAN HIS BODY FOR INJURIES.

YES. WHERE DO YOU WANT ME TO PUT THIS GUY?

GEORDI--DO YOU FIND IT ODD THAT THIS HUGE MACHINE ONLY HAD ONE MAN AT THE CONTROLS?

IT DOES SEEM A LITTLE WEIRD THAT ALL OF OUR PROBLEMS OF LATE ARE THIS GUY'S FAU--

DROP HIM, STRANGER--

-- DROP HIM AND BACK OFF...

NOW!

AAAH, REINFORCEMENTS!

NOW THAT'S MORE LIKE IT!

I'LL DO AS THEY SAY--

--BUT THEY HAVEN'T SAID ANYTHING ABOUT PICKING UP OUR *PHASERS*!

DATA, NO!

YOUR ATTACK JUST SERVED TO MAKE THE THELUVIANS MAD!

BEE-YOW

P-ZING

I KNOW--

--BUT AT LEAST THEY'RE MAD AT *ME!*

BRA-KOW

DATA'S RIGHT, GEORDI--

32

39

--HIS ACTIONS HAVE DRAWN ALL THE ENEMY'S ATTENTION!

GIVING US TIME TO TAKE COVER!

AND HE'S HEADING FOR THE OPEN HATCH OF THE HELLBLAZER...

"I JUST HOPE DATA CAN PULL OFF WHATEVER HE'S GOT PLANNED!"

HMMM... HIGHLY SOPHISTICATED WORKINGS... MOST ELABORATE I'VE EVER SEEN...

THIS MAY TAKE LONGER TO FIGURE OUT THAN I FIRST THOUGHT...

TIK TAKA TIK

ALL RIGHT... I'VE GOT IT NOW...

LOOK OUT! RUN!

CHOOOM

THEY'VE TURNED OUR OWN WEAPON UPON US!

SURRENDER YOUR WEAPONS TO US--

--OR YOU'LL FACE ANOTHER DOSE OF YOUR OWN MEDICINE!

NO, PLEASE-- WE GIVE!

NICE WORK, GANG-- MOVE IN!

THESE ARMS ARE FANTASTIC--TREMENDOUS PIECES OF WORK, TASHA!

WHO ARE YOU?

WHAT--?

LET US GO... OR WE'LL TELL!

33

CAPTAIN PICARD--

--I'VE GOT THEM!

I'VE LOCATED THE AWAY TEAM...

WHATEVER WAS INTERFERING WITH OUR COMPUTER HAS VANISHED!

EXCELLENT... I'M NOT ONE TO LOOK A GIFT HORSE IN THE MOUTH, SO...

LOCK ONTO THE ENTIRE TEAM AND BEAM THEM BACK TO THE ENTERPRISE... *IMMEDIATELY!*

THAT WILL NOT BE NECESSARY, CAPTAIN OF VISITORS--WE, TOO, HAVE LOCATED YOUR LANDING CREW...

...AS WELL AS THE TROUBLEMAKERS WHO'VE CAUSED THIS PROBLEM! A *PUNISHER* HAS BEEN DISPATCHED!

WE ASSURE YOU NO HARM WILL BEFALL YOUR PEOPLE.

SIR?

YOUR ORDER?

DO NOTHING, LT. BICKLEY.

I TRUST COMMANDER RIKER TO GUIDE THE TEAM THROUGH ANYTHING THAT LIES AHEAD--

--I CANNOT RISK AN INTER-GALACTIC INCIDENT.

IF IT WERE ONLY ME AND NOT THEM.

35

EASY NOW, FRIEND... THIS WILL NOT HURT...

I MIGHT BE ABLE TO HELP YOU...

REALLY--?

PLEASE... WE DIDN'T MEAN IT... WE SWEAR...

RELAX... YOU MUST RELA--

YES... I CAN FEEL IT...

IT IS AS I SUSPECTED...

THEY MEANT NO HARM.

THESE PEOPLE ARE SIMPLY *PLAYING!*

JUST A WAR-GAME!

PLEASE DON'T TELL ON US!

WE'LL BE *PUNISHED!*

DEANNA--?

I--I AM ALL RIGHT, WILLIAM...

GLAD *YOU'RE* OKAY, DEANNA-- BUT I THINK THE REST OF US ARE IN FOR IT NOW!

NOT QUITE AS GOOD AS DATA, TASHA-- BUT THAT IS ABOUT THE SIZE OF IT!

WHAT DO YOU MEAN, GEORDI? HAVE YOU PICKED UP SOMETH--

HOLY--!

ATTENTION. ATTENTION. STAND BY FOR TRANSPORTATION.

36

--CHILDREN.

PLEASE, STEP CLOSER-- MY PEOPLE ARE ANXIOUS TO WORK WITH YOUR PEOPLE TOWARDS THE GOAL OF PEACEFUL CO-EXISTENCE.

WE HAVE NOT HAD A WAR HERE IN CENTURIES-- DESPITE THE FACT THAT THE YOUNG ONES STILL LIKE TO PLAY AT IT.

A SAD STATEMENT, IN A WAY, ABOUT OUR SOCIETY.

SEEMS A FAIRLY NORMAL STATE- MENT JUDGING FROM THE WORLDS WE'VE SEEN.

YOU MEAN THEY AGE BACK- WARDS?

YES. MUCH LIKE THE MERLIN OF EARTH LEGEND--ACCORDING TO MY MEMORY BANKS.

I DO SO LOOK FORWARD TO DEALING WITH YOUR CAPTAIN-- --HE SHOWED ADMIRABLE RESTRAINT, WHEN OTHERS WOULD NOT HAVE. I RESPECT THE MAN-- CAN YOU SUMMON HIM?

I CERTAINLY CAN AND WILL, MY FRIEND... COMMANDER RIKER TO ENTERPRISE...

MISTER MOEZER, YOU HAVE THE COORDINATES DICTATED BY COMMANDER RIKER?

I DO, CAPTAIN.

EXCELLENT-- ENERGIZE...

CAPTAIN PICARD-- WAIT!

DO YOU THINK THAT I COULD MAYBE ONE DAY GO ON ONE OF THESE SAFE DIPLOMATIC- TYPE AWAY MISSIONS?

WESLEY, THESE TRIPS ARE ABSOLUTELY NO PLACE FOR--

--CHILDREN?

UNLESS, OF COURSE...

END

45

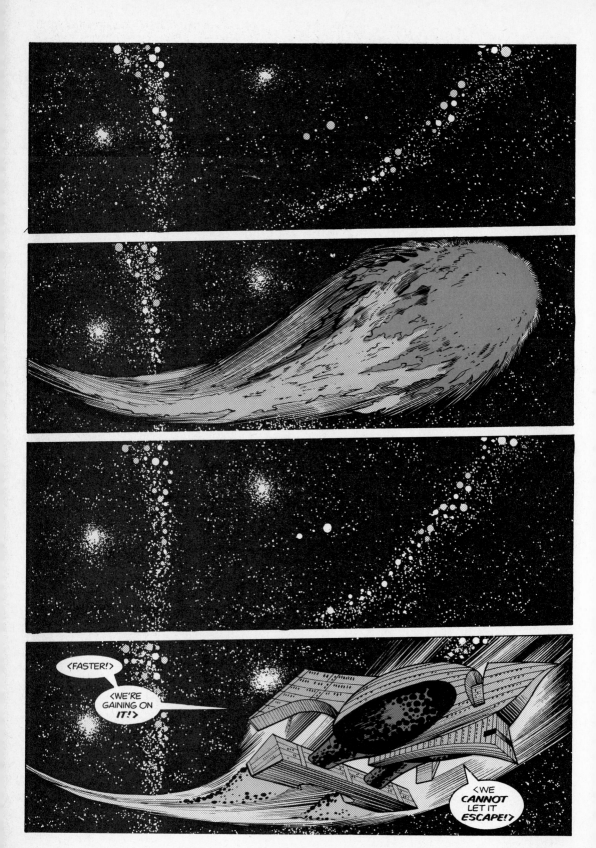

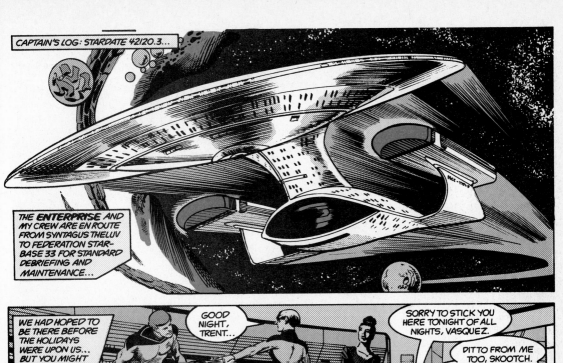

CAPTAIN'S LOG: STARDATE 42120.3...

THE **ENTERPRISE** AND MY CREW ARE EN ROUTE FROM SYNTAGUS THELUV TO FEDERATION STAR-BASE 33 FOR STANDARD DEBRIEFING AND MAINTENANCE...

WE HAD HOPED TO BE THERE BEFORE THE HOLIDAYS WERE UPON US... BUT YOU MIGHT SAY THAT FATE'S LIGHTS HAVE BEEN AGAINST US MOST OF THE WAY.

GOOD NIGHT, TRENT...

SORRY TO STICK YOU HERE TONIGHT OF ALL NIGHTS, VASQUEZ.

DITTO FROM ME TOO, SKOOTCH. DID I USE THAT SLANG PHRASE CORRECTLY?

YES, **DATA**--YOU'RE DOING VERY WELL.

THANK YOU, CAPTAIN... I DO NOT ANTICIPATE ANY PROBLEMS TONIGHT-- IT'S TRADITIONALLY A QUIET EVENING... GALAXY WIDE.

COMMANDER **RIKER**, YOU HAVE THE BRIDGE.

HAVE FUN, **GEORDI**, DATA. WE'LL TRY NOT TO FALL ASLEEP AT THE WHEEL HERE!

ENJOY THE PARTIES, SIR.

FRANKLY, RIKER, I HAVE LITTLE TOLERANCE FOR HOLIDAYS AND FESTIVITIES...

BUT THE CREW LIKES IT AND I SHOULD MAKE MY "APPEARANCE."

AREN'T YOU COMING, **WORF?**

SORRY, COUNSELOR **TROI**... BUT I CAN USE THE EXTRA TIME AT MY STATION. EVEN THOUGH MY KLINGON PEOPLE CELEBRATE THE COMING OF OUR GODS THIS SEASON AS WELL.

OH, WELL... HAPPY HOLIDAY TO YOU IN ANY EVENT...

HOLD THE TURBO-LIFT, SIR--WE'RE COMING...

2

GOOD NIGHT, ALL-- HAVE FUN WITH-OUT US.

AYE, AYE, SIR...

YOU, TOO.

HUMOR?.

COMMANDER RIKER...I'VE PICKED UP AN ALIEN READING ON MY PANEL.

REALLY...?

WORF--?

LOOKS INTERESTING, SIR...

UNCATEGORIZED ALIEN VESSEL ENTERING AT THE EQUIVALENT OF OUR WARP FACTOR TWO.

HMMM...

...ROUTINE DIPLOMATIC OVERTURES ARE IN ORDER, I'D SAY.

NO PROBLEM, CAPTAIN PICARD...ENJOY YOURSELVES.

AS I'VE ALREADY TOLD YOU, COMMANDER... THAT IS HIGHLY UNLIKELY.

WELL, I'LL HAVE ONE FOR YOU, SIR.

SO LONG.

TRENT, SKOOTCH... OPTIMUM MAGNIFICATION OF SHIP ON THE VIEWSCREEN.

WORF... MAKE INITIAL CONTACT.

AYE, SIR--

--OPENING ALL HAILING FREQUENCIES FOR COMMUNICATION.

THE SPIRIT OF THE SEASON OUGHT TO KEEP THIS MEETING ON THE CONGENIAL SIDE, EH, MEN?

WHAT IF THIS ISN'T CHRISTMAS TIME FOR THOSE GUYS, SIR?

3

I DON'T LIKE THIS.

SIR, THERE'S ABSOLUTELY NO CAUSE TO ALARM ANYONE... YET.

AND YOUR ABSENCE FROM TONIGHT'S FUNCTIONS MIGHT CAUSE JUST THAT.

DEANNA'S RIGHT, SIR... BESIDES, INTERRUPTIONS IN POWER LIKE THAT-- WHILE RARE--ARE NOT UNHEARD OF.

I WOULD LIKE TO SPEAK WITH THE ALIEN COMMANDER, WORF--

--BRING HIM ON AND HAVE THE COMPUTER TRANSLATE HIS LANGUAGE FOR ME.

AYE, SIR... HERE IS A...CAPTAIN *BRONDER*...

GREETINGS. I AM COMMANDER RIKER OF THE U.S.S. ENTERPRISE, CAPTAIN BRONDER.

THE APOLOGIES OF MY PEOPLE, COMMANDER OF THE ENTERPRISE--

--WE WILL HOLD OUR POSITION TO AVOID ANY FURTHER DISTURBANCES, LIKE THOSE YOUR FELLOW WORF DESCRIBED TO US.

SCANNED 'EM, SIR--THEY SEEM PRETTY HARMLESS.

ALLOW ME TO EXTEND THE FEDERATION'S INVITATION, BRONDER, TO YOU AND SEVERAL OF YOUR PEOPLE'S REPRESENTATIVES--

--TO *JOIN US* IN OUR SEASON OF CELEBRATION...

ALL IN AN EFFORT TO SHARE THE WAYS OF OUR PEOPLES WITH EACH OTHER.

OF COURSE, YOU MUST BOARD OUR VESSEL UNARMED.

THAT WOULD BE WITHOUT NEED OF SPEAKING IT, RIKER.

WE ACCEPT YOUR GENEROUS INVITATION, RIKER--AND WE LOOK FORWARD TO ABSORBING ALL WE CAN FROM YOUR KIND.

VERY WELL, PREPARE TO BE TELEPORTED IN THE NEXT THIRTY STANDARD MINUTES.

ENTERPRISE OUT.

GIVE HIM A FEW MINUTES, WORF--AND THEN CONTACT CAPTAIN PICARD.

AYE, SIR.

6

I DID SENSE SOMETHING *UNUSUAL* BACK IN THE TURBO-LIFT...

...BUT WAS IT NECESSARILY SOMETHING TO BE *WORRIED* ABOUT?

IF ONLY THE BETAZOID PART OF MY HERITAGE WOULD ALLOW ME MORE CERTAINTY.

BRIDGE TO CAPTAIN PICARD. REQUESTING YOUR PRESENCE IN TRANS-PORTER ROOM 6...

...TO WELCOME DIPLOMATIC ENTOURAGE FROM ALIEN VESSEL--THEY'VE EXPRESSED AN INTEREST IN JOINING OUR CELEBRATIONS.

ACKNOWLEDGED, MISTER WORF.

IT WILL BE GOOD TO STALL THOSE PARTIES A MOMENT--

--THOUGH I FEEL NOW I SHOULD HAVE STAYED ON THE BRIDGE.

I'VE ALWAYS LONGED TO HAVE THE HOLIDAYS BACK IN MY LIFE...

I DIDN'T GET TO DO MUCH CELEBRATING WHEN I WAS A CHILD ON THE *COLONY*...

AND MY DUTIES WITH THE FEDERATION SINCE HAVE KEPT ME FROM KEEPING MY FAITH...

I'M REALLY LOOKING FORWARD TO LOOSENING UP TONIGHT!

OH, MRS. *BICKLEY*...

IS THE TANTRUM OF THE HOUR OVER FOR NOW?

THINK MAYBE WE COULD CELEBRATE *ONE* CHRISTMAS ON TIME FOR A CHANGE?

GO ON AHEAD, MICHAEL J. BICKLEY, GO AHEAD--

--SINCE IT'S QUITE OBVIOUS THAT YOU CAN'T WAIT TO HIT THAT CHRISTMAS CHEER FOR ANOTHER FIVE MINUTES!

BUT, MA...! DO I HAVE TO GO TO THIS DULL OLD PARTY?

IT'S NOT LIKE I *BELIEVE* IN ANY ONE OF THESE ANCIENT RITUALS--CHRISTMAS, CHANUKAH, RETHLUME, OR ANY-THING!

WESLEY CRUSHER-- YOU ARE ACCOMPANYING ME TO THE PARTY!

NOW MOVE IT!

BUT I'M ALWAYS NERVOUS AT HUMAN GATHERINGS, GEORDI!

AS AN ANDROID, I'M STILL HAVING TROUBLE *UNDER-STANDING* ACCEPTED BEHAVIOR DURING THESE OBSERVATIONS OF ARCHAIC CUSTOMS.

YOU LOOK FINE, DATA-- NOW JUST RELAX!

NONSENSE, BUDDY--JUST FOLLOW MY LEAD WHEN WE GET INTO THE HOLO-CHAMBER.

7

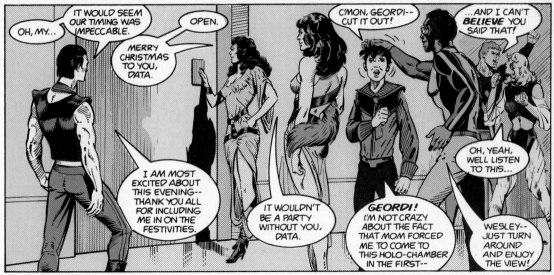

THANK YOU FOR POSTPONING YOUR RECREATION TIME, TASHA.

WHEN I HEARD YOUR PAGE--I THOUGHT I COULD BE OF SERVICE.

FIVE READY TO BEAM ABOARD, CAPTAIN.

ENERGIZE, MISTER FOREST.

WELCOME ABOARD THE U.S.S. ENTERPRISE... I AM CAPTAIN JEAN-LUC PICARD.

AND I AM BRONDER OF THE CREEG. MAY WE SEE MORE OF YOUR MAGNIFICENT SHIP?

IT IS OUR CUSTOM TO SHAKE HANDS WHEN--

CAPTAIN-- IF I MAY-- IT MUST NOT BE THEIR WAY.

ONE WOULD ASSUME.

BUT IT IS CHRISTMAS, AFTER ALL...

GENTLEMEN-- IF YOU'LL WALK THIS WAY...

9

YOUR MEN SEEM VERY IMPRESSED WITH THE ENTERPRISE, BRONDER...

THEY CERTAINLY ARE TAKING IN EVERY INCH OF THIS CORRIDOR...

MOM'S BUSY... NOW'S MY CHANCE...

THEY'LL BE SHORT-HANDED ON THE BRIDGE WHAT WITH ALL OF THESE PARTIES TONIGHT--

--MAYBE I CAN GET COMMANDER RIKER TO LET ME SIT AT THE OP POST AGAIN.

WELL, IF YOU CREEG LIKE OUR HALLWAYS--

SOMEONE'S COMING!

BETTER POUR IT ON!

--YOU REALLY OUGHT TO ENJOY OUR FIRST STOP!

MANY WHO VISIT MY SHIP ASK TO SEE OUR FAMOUS HOLO-DECKS, BRONDER--

--SO WON'T YOU AND YOUR PEOPLE JOIN US IN OUR HOLIDAY CELEBRATING?

YES.

I FELT IT!

IT IS HERE!

OR IT HAS BEEN RECENTLY.

I CAN SENSE ITS ENERGY TRAIL...

10

IT'S COME DOWN THIS CORRIDOR...

YES! IT'S JUST AROUND THAT--

--BEND!

HUH?

HEY--! WHO'RE YOU?!

DID MY MOTHER SEND YOU TO--

BAH...

...YOU ARE NOT THE ONE I'M AFTER!

I MUST HAVE MISREAD YOUR FORCE-AURA!

WHAT WAS THAT ALL ABOUT?

MORE IMPORTANTLY, WHAT WAS THAT?

HMMMM.

HE'S HEADING BACK TOWARDS THE HOLO-DECK-- I'D BETTER FOLLOW...

BRONDER, OUR SHIP'S COUNSELOR, DEANNA TROI...

AND LIEUTENANT GEORDI LAFORGE.

WELCOME ABOARD, SIR.

MORE ALIENS LIKE THE ONE I FOLLOWED...

BUT WHY WAS THAT ONE WALKING AROUND THE ENTERPRISE UNESCORTED?

I'VE GOT TO TALK TO CAPTAIN PICARD!

11

CAPTAIN PICARD-- I *MUST* SPEAK WITH YOU.

WESLEY, PLEASE... NOT NOW.

BUT, SIR, ONE OF THESE ALIENS WAS WANDERING THE HALLS *ALONE,* AND REGULATION TX 99.43 CLEARLY STATES--

WESLEY, A LITTLE RESPECT FOR OUR VISITORS MIGHT BE IN ORDER.

BUT, SIR... THIS ONE HERE WAS FOLLOWING ME IN THE HALL...

AND HE SEEMED UPSET WHEN I CAUGHT HIM AND HE SAID I "WASN'T THE ONE HE WAS LOOKING FOR."

"LOOKING FOR?"

IS THAT TRUE, BRONDER? ARE YOU CREEG HERE *LOOKING* FOR SOMEONE?

WELL, CAPTAIN, NOT EXACTLY SOME*ONE*.

AREN'T WE *ALL* SEARCHING FOR THAT *ENTITY*... THE ONE WE TRY TO MODEL ALL OUR ACTIONS AFTER...

OUR *INSPIRATION?*

WHAT *ARE* YOU ON ABOUT, BRONDER?

WAIT A MOMENT, CAPTAIN. BRONDER, DO YOU BELIEVE THE BEING-- OR *FORCE*--YOU'RE SPEAKING OF IS *HERE?*

"YES. WE WERE ON THE TRAIL OF *SOMETHING* WHEN OUR INSTRUMENTS LED US TO YOUR SHIP."

SIR, IF THIS BEING ENTERED OUR SHIP, THAT MIGHT HELP EXPLAIN THAT STRANGE POWER SURGE EARLIER.

HMMM. VERY WELL, DATA--

--YOU AND LAFORGE SCAN THIS DECK.

AYE, SIR.

12

I'M AFRAID I DETECT NOTHING OUT OF THE ORDINARY, SIR-- EXCEPT FOR THE CREEG, OF COURSE.

SAME HERE, SIR--NO BEING, ENTITY *OR* FORCE.

THEN PERHAPS WE WERE MISTAKEN AS WELL.

BETTER LUCK NEXT TIME, LITTLE TROUBLESHOOTER.

NO.

THERE *IS* SOMETHING FUNNY GOING ON HERE--

--WHY DON'T YOU *BELIEVE* ME?

WAIT, BEVERLY...

WESLEY, COME BACK HERE...

YOU STAY... ENJOY THE PARTY.

I'LL CALM WESLEY DOWN.

WESLEY, WAIT.

COUNSELOR?

I'D LIKE TO TALK TO YOU--

--ABOUT WHAT *YOU* THINK THESE VISITORS ARE UP TO.

BECAUSE I *FELT* IT IN THERE.

IT WAS ONE OF THE STRONGEST FORCES I'VE EVER "TOUCHED."

BUT... EVEN IF YOU BELIEVE ME-- WHAT CAN WE DO?

WE HAVE NO *PROOF* THAT THEY'RE UP TO ANY--

COUNSELOR... DID YOU JUST HEAR SOMETHING?

QUIET, WESLEY, I THINK IT'S--

13

IT'S TOO LATE FOR SILENCE!

YOU, WOMAN, YOU HAVE SENSED THE POWER AS WE DID!

AND NOW YOU WILL FIND IT FOR US!

BECAUSE WE ARE HERE TO *TAKE* THE SPIRIT FROM YOU!

COMMANDER RIKER...

WE'VE GOT SOME TROUBLE.

WHAT IS IT, SKOOCH?

I'M REGISTERING SOME SLIGHT ENERGY DRAINS ON MY CONSOLE, SIR.

IT LOOKS LIKE IT MAY HAVE SOMETHING TO DO WITH THE ALIEN SHIP.

JUST IN CASE IT IS THE CREEG, SKOOCH, THROW UP OUR SHIELDS TO PREVENT--

TOO LATE, SIR.

14

THE LIGHTS--!

C'MON, DEANNA-- NOW'S OUR CHANCE!

OOOOF!

BONK

HEY! I DID IT!

MAYBE NOW I CAN FIND OUT THE CREEG'S TRUE MOTIVATION.

DAMN. I CANNOT "READ" HIM THROUGH ALL OF HIS COVERING!

WAIT, DEANNA--HIS EYE-OPENINGS!

YES, I CAN "FEEL" HIS INTENTIONS VERY CLEARLY NOW!

AND THEY ARE NOT GOOD!

NO!

YOU CANNOT STEAL MY FORCE FROM ME!

I MUST REACH BRONDER!

OHHH.

HURRY, WESLEY--

--WE MUST STOP HIM!

BRONDER--

--THEY'VE TRIED TO DRAIN ME! THEY ARE LIKE US!

HUH?

WHAT--?

15

IF OUR INTENT IS KNOWN--

--THEN THERE IS NO NEED FOR FALSE DIPLOMACY ANY LONGER!

WEAPONS--

--BEAMED FROM THEIR SHIP!

TAKE 'EM, GEORDI!

WAY AHEAD OF YOU, TASHA!

HOLD YOURSELVES, CREEG!

EVEN WITHOUT POWER, WE OUTNUMBER YOU A HUNDRED TO ONE IN THIS ROOM ALONE!

MY CREW HAS ALREADY DISARMED THREE OF YOU!

BESIDES, WE DO **NOT** HAVE THE ENTITY YOU ARE LOOKING FOR!

SORRY, SIR... BUT IT **IS** HERE-- I FELT IT!

YEAH, AND SHE READ ONE OF THESE CREEG GUYS AND THEY'RE BAD NEWS!

WESLEY...?

VERY WELL...

...WE WERE WRONG TO TRY TO TRICK YOU. OUR INSTRUMENTS DETECTED THE ENTITY HERE IN THIS SECTOR--

--BUT WHILE THE ENTERPRISE'S INSTRUMENTS APPARENTLY MISSED IT... YOUR TROI SEEMS TO BE ABLE TO HOME IN ON WHEREVER IT IS!

MY **BETAZOID** GIFTS ARE NOT ALWAYS ONE HUNDRED PERCENT ACCURATE--

--BUT THE SPIRIT I SENSED **WAS** ONE OF THE MOST **POWERFUL** I'VE EVER ENCOUNTERED!

16

SO IF THIS THING'S SO POWERFUL, WHERE IS IT N--?

HOLY--! DATA?

DATA!

IT WAS *INSIDE* DATA!

MY VISOR IS PICKING IT UP AS IT'S LEAVING HIM!

I MUST BE THE ONLY ONE THAT CAN "SEE" IT!

IT-- IT LOOKS LIKE A... LIKE A SKINNY OLD MAN!

IT *IS* HERE!

UNSHIELD YOURSELVES, CREEG!

READY FOR *INTAKE*, BRONDER!

17

COMMENCE! BRING THE SPIRIT TOWARDS US!

THIS IS ALL SO STRANGE--

--I CANNOT SEE ANYTHING!

I ASSURE YOU, SIR-- SEEING IS BELIEVING!

I CANNOT SEE IT, GEORDI-- BUT I BELIEVE IT'S THERE!

I BELIEVE TOO!

WELL, THEN SEE IF YOU CAN ALL BELIEVE THIS...

THE ENTITY IS... IT'S GAINING MASS!

SOMEHOW IT'S GROWING...RIGHT BEFORE MY VISOR!

CAPTAIN... CAPTAIN...

...THE SPIRIT IS GOING TO ATTACK BRONDER!

YARRRR!

63

GEORDI, WHERE IS IT--I CAN'T SEE IT!

IT'S *INSIDE* BRONDER--

NO, WAIT!

IT'S *LEAVING* BRONDER--AND THE ROOM!

LAFORGE, LEAD YAR AND TROI AFTER *IT,* I'LL--

NO!

I MEAN--WAIT, PLEASE, SIR. PLEASE LET IT GO! IT MEANS NO HARM! I KNOW... IT WAS... INSIDE ME!

IT'S JUST SPREADING--

--SPREADING--

--WELL, IT FELT *WONDERFUL!*

WELL, IF THEY'RE NOT GOING AFTER IT--*WE ARE!*

HALT! I'M CAPTAIN OF THIS VESSEL, AND I'LL DECIDE--

FROLAG, *STOP!*

CAPTAIN PICARD'S RIGHT.

THIS IS *HIS* SHIP--*WE* ARE THE GUESTS--WE'LL DO AS HE SAYS!

BRONDER... IF YOU'RE TRYING TO--

CAPTAIN--

--IT *WAS* WONDERFUL!

19

WELL THEN, CREEG--

--IF ANYONE IS TO FIND THIS THING, WE'LL NEED OUR POWER RESTORED!

WHAT?!

YOU HEARD CAPTAIN BRONDER'S ORDER, CHILP--

--RESTORE POWER TO THE ALIEN VESSEL!

IT JUST DOESN'T SOUND LIKE BRONDER TO RELINQUISH STOLEN ENERGIES...

SOMETHING MUST'VE GOTTEN INTO HIM DOWN THERE!

POWER'S ON.

YOU OKAY, TOO, BUDDY?

YES.

THEN LET'S FIND THAT SPOOK!

QUICKLY, GEORDI--

--YOU, DEANNA AND THE CREEG MUST POOL YOUR SENSES AND--

WAIT, SIR... LET'S TRY HOLO-DECK 3, TO THE LEFT...

YES... I'M DEFINITELY SCANNING SOME FORM OF ENERGY TRAIL.

A QUICK PEEK IN ON THIS DECK'S PARTY OUGHTA--

20

MAN, THESE MARCIAK CREWMEMBERS REALLY KNOW HOW TO CELEBRATE THE--

GEORDI, THE SPIRIT?

SORRY, SIR...

...IT HAS COME BY HERE... BUT IT'S NOT HERE NOW.

ONWARD, THEN.

I SENSE IT STRONGLY HERE, GEORDI LAFORGE?

YES, BRONDER... IT SEEMS TO DISSIPATE ENERGY AS IT TRAVELS.

NO. IT'S NOT HERE AT TREMPOLIAN TRIAKK PARTY...

...BUT IT'S LEFT ITS ESSENCE.

BRONDER...THE SPIRIT ENTERED YOU AS WELL...

CAN YOU STILL FEEL A PART OF IT WITHIN YOU?

YES, DATA... BUT...

DO YOU TOO HAVE THE FEELING OF WHERE IT MIGHT BE NOW?

SHIP'S NORTH!

21

THE BRIDGE!

HURRY!

ALIEN SHIP MAINTAINING, SKOOCH?

PRACTICALLY DEAD AS A DOORNAIL, SIR.

I'M NOT EVEN SURE IF IT WAS THEM GEESING OUR POWER BEFORE ANYMORE.

WONDER IF THAT BLACKOUT HAD ANY ILL EFFECTS ON THOSE PARTIES WE'RE NOT AT?

SPOSE WE COULD CALL THE--

--CAPTAIN?

WELL, GEORDI-- IS IT HERE?

IS WHAT HERE?

YESSIR-- IT'S HERE--

--BUT IT LOOKS DISSIPATED--TIRED ALMOST.

THEN I MUST HAVE IT!

NO! DATA, GRAB HIM!

HE'S SUCKING IN THE ENTITY'S LIFE FORCE, BRONDER--

FROLAG, STOP!

IT'S DYING-- NEEDS OUR HELP...

...OUR LOVE.

ISN'T THAT THE LEAST WE CAN OFFER IT?

AFTER WHAT IT HAS DONE FOR US?

22

HEY--! IT'S...IT'S GETTING UP!

YOU GUYS'RE *HELPING* IT!

SIR, IF I MAY BE SO BOLD-- WHAT THE HELL'S GOING ON AROUND HERE?

WILL...I CAN'T SAY I'M *TOTALLY* SURE--BUT I'M TEMPTED TO SAY SOMETHING *SPIRITUAL!*

JEAN-LUC, ARE YOU SAYING--?

EVEN THE CAPTAIN BELIEVES IN IT!

IT'S THRIVING, SIR--ON OUR *FEELINGS!*

--AND IT LOOKS LIKE IT WANTS TO--

--PAY US BACK!

OOOH!

EEEEOOO!

WOOOGH!

AAAHH!

IT'S GONE, SIR! I CAN FEEL IT!

I THINK WE ALL CAN... NOW.

I--I DON'T KNO--OH--OHHH-- JUST SIGNAL, BRONDER ON THE ALIEN SHIP...

DRILGE, WHAT'S THIS *FEELI--?* OOOOPH!

CAPTAIN PICARD, I HAVE A SIGNAL ON MY COMMUNICATOR--FROM THE CREEG... THEY SAY THEY'D LIKE TO *JOIN* OUR CELEBRATIONS! THEY ALSO MENTIONED SOMETHING ABOUT *GIFTS!*

WELL THEN BY ALL MEANS, LIEUTENANT WORF-- WAVE THEM ON!

CAPTAIN'S LOG: STARDATE 42122.7...

WHATEVER THE GALAXY TRAVELING ENTITY WE ENCOUNTERED WAS...

...IT LEFT BOTH THE ENTERPRISE AND CREEG CREWS WITH MORE-- MUCH MORE THAN WE COULD'VE EVER GIVEN IT.

I ONLY HOPE IT LASTS INTO THE NEW YEAR.

23

STAR TREK
THE NEXT GENERATION

CAPTAIN'S LOG STARDATE 42125.7...

HAVING SUCCESSFULLY INTRODUCED THE CREEG--A RACE OF ENERGY SIPHONS--TO OUR FEDERATION ON TAROD--

--THE ENTERPRISE MAKES ITS WAY ON IMPULSE POWER TO FALTOS, THE FIRST PLANET OUTSIDE THE CHARTED PERIPHERY OF SECTOR 902.

THAT IS, OF COURSE, ASSUMING THAT FALTOS EXISTS AT ALL. SHE HAS ALWAYS BEEN MORE LEGEND THAN CERTAINTY.

EMBARKING ON A NEWLY ISSUED ASSIGNMENT ALWAYS LEADS TO A MIXTURE OF EMOTIONS FOR MY CREW-- MOST PARADOXICALLY, ANTICIPATION *AND* TREPIDATION...

NEVER *KNOWING*, YET *NEEDING* TO KNOW, WHAT LIES AHEAD DRIVES US--AND CAUTION, GOVERNED BY REASON, KEEPS US RETURNING HOME TIME AFTER TIME.

BUT TO DO ANY GOOD AT ALL IN THIS DAY AND AGE, THE FEDERATION *NEEDS* FACTUAL INFORMATION-- AND IT'S OUR JOB TO BRING IT BACK.

IN THIS INSTANCE, FALTOS IS THE UNKNOWN WHICH LIES AHEAD--AND, BARRING ANY SIDE-TRACKING, THE ENTERPRISE WILL BE ABLE TO TELL THE FEDERATION WHAT IT *NEEDS* TO KNOW BY 42150.

G-3613

FACTOR Q

MIKE CARLIN
WRITER
PABLO MARCOS
PENCILLER
CARLOS GARZON & ARNE STARR
INKERS
BOB PINAHA
LETTERER
CARL GAFFORD
COLORIST
ROBERT GREENBERGER
EDITOR

UH--

--oh.

VERY ENTERTAINING, LIEUTENANT YAR.

AN AWARD WINNING DEATH SCENE IF EVER I'VE SEEN ONE!

CAPTAIN PICARD!

SIR.

LET ME EXPLAIN, SIR...

I HAD EVERY INTENTION TO.

I WAS ONLY PLAYING WITH YOUNG WESLEY, SIR...

AND I KNOW I SHOULD KNOW BETTER, BUT...YOU DID ORDER WESLEY TO LEARN EVERY ASPECT OF THE SHIP...AND, WELL, SECURITY MANEUVERS ARE IMPORTANT...

AND BESIDES, I NEVER REALLY GOT A CHANCE TO PLAY MUCH WHEN I WAS A CHILD AND I DIDN'T WANT WESLEY TO--

THAT'S ENOUGH, TASHA.

AS FEDERATION OFFICERS, WE ARE RESPONSIBLE FOR THE SAFETY AND WELL-BEING OF A THOUSAND CIVILIAN PASSENGERS ON BOARD THE ENTERPRISE.

AND, DESPITE NOBLE INTENTIONS, SOMEONE COULD HAVE EASILY BEEN INJURED THE WAY YOU TWO WERE RUNNING AROUND.

A SECURITY CHIEF MIGHT DO LESS DAMAGE TO THE SHIP AND HER REPUTATION "PLAYING" ON ONE OF THE SHIP'S HOLO-DECKS.

BUT, SIR...THE PHASERS WEREN'T EVEN--

FRANKLY, I DON'T KNOW MANY HELMSMEN WHO'D CONDUCT THEM-SELVES SO POORLY EITHER.

SORRY, SIR.

IT WON'T HAPPEN AGAIN, SIR.

I'M POSITIVE IT WILL NOT.

BOY, WE REALLY BLEW IT, HUH, TASHA?

WE'D BETTER MOVE ALONG, WESLEY.

OKAY, TASHA, BUT--

-- CAN I ASK YOU SOMETHING ON THE WAY BACK TO MOM'S OFFICE IN SICK-BAY?

SURE, WES.

DIDN'T YOU HAVE ANY *FRIENDS* WHEN YOU WERE MY AGE?

OH, BECAUSE I TOLD THE CAPTAIN I HADN'T *PLAYED* MUCH AS A GIRL... WELL, I DIDN'T GROW UP IN AN ENVIRONMENT LIKE THE ONE YOU'RE USED TO, WESLEY.

AND, NO, I DIDN'T REALLY HAVE MANY FRIENDS WHEN I WAS ON THE COLONY.

"BUT I DID HAVE SOMETHING THERE I HOPE YOU NEVER HAVE...

"ENEMIES.

"ON THE SETTLEMENT IT SEEMED EVERYONE WAS AGAINST ME...

"AND EVERY*THING!*

"SOUNDS LIKE A NORMAL TEEN-AGER'S ANXIETIES WHEN I SAY IT NOW, I GUESS...

"THAT COLONY WAS A *PIT* -- A MALEVOLENT, BREEDING GROUND FOR UNPRINCIPLED, BLACK-HEARTED IMMORALITY.

"BUT, NO, I WAS NOT LIKE *THEM!*

"NARCOTICS DEALERS, SLAVE DEALERS, TREMBLING WOMEN...YOU NAME IT -- AND THIS PLACE WAS TOPS IN ITS FIELD!

"FOR A WHILE--THAT SEEMED LIKE FOREVER--I *TRIED* TO FIT IN. AND NO MATTER WHAT I DID, OR WHERE I WENT, I ALWAYS ENDED UP ANTAGONIZING SOMEONE.

"I WAS CONSTANTLY ON THE RUN-- FROM THE STREET GANGS, FROM THE DEALERS, FROM *MYSELF!*

"AND IF THERE WERE ANY LAW THERE, I'D HAVE BEEN ON THE RUN FROM THEM, TOO!

"I WAS *FORCED* BY THESE OPPRESSIVE INFLUENCES TO HIDE OUT--

"--UNTIL I FOUND THE MEANS TO MAKE MY ESCAPE *PERMANENT!*"

I'VE THANKED GOD FOR THE FEDERATION AND MY CAREER WITH THEM SINCE THEN. I SUPPOSE THAT THAT EXPERIENCE MADE ME A STRONGER PERSON SOMEHOW...

BUT I'D GIVE ANYTHING TO BE ABLE TO RUN FROM THOSE MEMORIES.

LIEUTENANT YAR. TO THE BRIDGE.

GOTTA GO, KIDDO. YOU OKAY?

YUP, SEE YOU, TASHA.

SORRY AGAIN FOR GETTING YOU IN HOT WATER WITH THE CAPTAIN.

5

CAPTAIN--?

THIS ISN'T ABOUT...?

NO, TASHA. NUMBER ONE, UPDATE THE LIEUTENANT.

WE'VE COME UPON A SHIP... OF UNCLASSIFIED ALIEN DESIGN...

AND WORF'S BEEN UNABLE TO RAISE ANYONE INSIDE OF IT ON EITHER AUDIO OR VIDEO.

BY SUMMONING YOU, TASHA, WE'RE MERELY PREPARING FOR THE WORST.

I SEE, COMMANDER RIKER--

--PERHAPS IF I...

NOTHING. I'M NOT REGISTERING ANY LIFE-FORMS ABOARD THE ALIEN VESSEL WITH MY SENSORS. NONE WHATSOEVER.

ALTHOUGH, COUNSELOR TROI TELLS US SHE CAN FEEL SOMETHING THERE--SOMETHING WRONG.

PRECISELY WHY WE'RE STUMPED...

MY FIRST INSTINCT WOULD BE TO HAVE AN AWAY TEAM INVESTIGATE THE SHIP FIRSTHAND...

BUT THERE IS DANGER...

6

I WOULD LIKE TO VOLUNTEER, SIR...

I'D RATHER GET IN THERE, THAN BACK OFF, SIR.

I'M WITH TASHA, SIR-- I'D LIKE TO GO AS WELL.

DEANNA?

IT DOES APPEAR TO BE OUR ONLY OPTION AT THIS POINT.

VERY WELL. NATASHA, WILL...TO THE TRANSPORTER ROOM IMMEDIATELY.

AYE, SIR.

MAY I RECOMMEND THAT SEVERAL MEMBERS OF TASHA'S SECURITY TEAM ACCOMPANY THEM, SIR?

GOOD IDEA, COUNSELOR.

INQUIRY CAPTAIN. PERHAPS GEORDI AND MYSELF COULD BE OF ASSISTANCE ON THIS MISSION?

YES.

THEY'VE BOTH PROVEN THEMSELVES VALUABLE ASSETS ON PREVIOUS MANEUVERS.

DATA? LAFORGE? *NO!*

YOU'RE *BOTH* GOING TO BE NEEDED *HERE!*

VERY WELL.

I GUESS.

SCARES ME WHEN SHE PULLS THAT *BETAZOID* PREDICTION STUFF.

OH, WELL...GUESS THEY GO WITHOUT US. NICE TRY THOUGH, DATA.

LOCK IN COORDINATES, ENSIGN TURNER.

AND PREPARE TO TRANSPORT.

ENERGIZE.

AYE, SIR. ENERGIZING.

7

IT'S DESERTED, COMMANDER.

AS OUR SENSORS INDICATED.

GIBSON, HAHN... SEARCH THE IMMEDIATE AREA FOR *ANY* SIGNS OF LIFE.

STRANGE...

WHY WOULD ANYONE *ABANDON* A SHIP LIKE THIS -- POWER ON, AND IN FINE WORKING ORDER -- OUT HERE IN THE MIDDLE OF NOWHERE?

AND WHERE WOULD THEY'VE GONE?

COULD THEY'VE BEEN RUNNING FROM *US*?

OR PERHAPS FROM SOMETHING WE'RE *MISSING* RIGHT HERE ON THEIR OWN--

K-RASSH-BDAKK

GIBSON? HAHN?

HURRY, SIR... DOWN THIS CORRIDOR!

RIKER TO ENTERPRISE.

COME IN, ENTERPRISE.

RIKER, SIR. I'M PIPING HIM THROUGH.

SOMETHING'S HAPPENING, SIR... DOESN'T *SOUND* GOOD... WE'RE INVESTIGATING... WILL KEEP ENTERPRISE POSTED...

CAPTAIN PICARD...

BRING THEM BACK, SIR... PLEASE.

YOUR READINGS ARE VALUED, DEANNA, AND ARE MORE OFTEN THAN NOT VERY ACCURATE... WE KEPT DATA AND LAFORGE HERE AT YOUR REQUEST.

BUT, RIGHT NOW, WE MUST *KNOW* WHAT WE'RE FACING.

AND SO FAR WE HAVE NO *EVIDENCE* THAT RIKER, YAR AND HER MEN CANNOT HANDLE THE SITUATION OVER THERE.

YES, SIR... I UNDERSTAND.

8

ENTERPRISE... BOTH GIBSON AND HAHN'RE DOWN...

I'LL SCAN THEM WITH MY 'CORDER.

NO SIGN OF ASSAILANTS.

VITAL SIGNS ARE READING OKAY, CAPTAIN...THEY'RE UNCONSCIOUS--

--BUT THEY'RE ALIVE.

WHAT COULD'VE HAPPENED TO THEM, THOUGH? IT ALMOST SEEMS AS IF THEY KNOCKED EACH OTHER OU--

WHACK!

COMMANDER!

SOMEONE-- SOMETHING-- HIT ME!

NOW IT'S-- =MMMMPH!=

COMMANDER-- THERE'S NOTHING THERE...!

=UFFF!=

STUN IT, TASHA! GET IT OFF!

I--I CAN'T!

I DON'T SEE ANY--! I MIGHT STUN YOU, SIR...

HANG ON, COMMANDER...I'LL TRY TO PHYSICALLY--

HURRY, TASHA...CAN'T B-BREATHE...IT'S TOO...TOO--

=UNNGH!=

WHUD!

COMMANDER?!

WILLIAM?!

9

OUT COLD.

THIS IS TASHA YAR OF THE U.S.S. ENTERPRISE... IDENTIFY YOURSELF!

SHOW YOURSELF BEFORE OUR CAPTAIN TAKES DRASTIC MEAS--

THUNNT

MY PHASER--!

YAR TO ENTERPRISE... COME IN, ENTER--

DO NOT DO ANYTHING RASH!

NO... NOT YOU! I--I...

WE HAD INTENDED TO REMAIN CLOAKED INDEFINITELY, BUT SINCE IT IS YOU, TASHA, DEAR...

...WE JUST COULDN'T PLAY GAMES WITH ONE OF OUR OLDEST FRIENDS!

P-PLEASE... LEAVE ME ALO-- OWWWW!

GOT HER, REG! NOW WHAT?

GET THEM BACK ON BOARD--NOW!

THERE IS GREAT FEAR AND HATE! THERE IS GRAVE DANGER THERE!

DEANNA--?

HELM...LOCK ONTO AWAY TEAM AND BEAM THEM BACK TO THE ENTERPRISE!

PRONTO!

NO! THEY'RE BEING TAKEN!

HEAR ME, TASHA--YOU CANNOT HIDE FROM US ANY LONGER!

WE WILL FIND YOU AGAIN!

10

FOUND ME... ALL THESE YEARS...

CAN'T HIDE...

NO HOPE... NOWHERE TO GO...

LIEUTENANT YAR...? TASHA?!

SHE'S IN A STATE OF SHOCK!

TURNER--CALL COUNSELOR TROI, IMMEDIATELY!

AYE, DOCTOR CRUSHER!

THAT WILL NOT BE NECESSARY, ENSIGN...

HOW IS SHE?

I WAS HOPING YOU WOULD BE ABLE TO TELL ME!

CAN YOU CHECK HER OUT, WHILE I TEND TO THE OTHERS?

EVEN THOUGH IT LOOKS LIKE THEY'RE SIMPLY UNCONSCIOUS-- THERE MAY BE INTERNAL DAMAGE.

I'M AFRAID I'M ALREADY SENSING SOME INTERNAL DAMAGE IN TASHA'S CASE!

EASY, TASHA... CALM DOWN AND TELL ME...

THEY'LL FIND ME... ALWAYS DID... ALWAYS WILL...

TASHA, I'M TRYING TO HELP YOU-- YOU MUST OPEN UP TO ME.

YOU MUST LET ME ALL THE WAY IN.

NO HOPE... NO HELP...

NOTHING. SHE'S BLOCKING.

THIS IS DOCTOR CRUSHER REQUESTING FOUR STRETCHERS IN TRANSPORTER D.

DO YOU MIND IF I ACCOMPANY YOU TO YOUR SICK BAY, DOCTOR?

DEANNA-- YOU READ MY MIND...

11

YOU ARE FIGHTING THE WRONG FIGHT, MY FRIEND--I AM SIMPLY TRYING TO *AID* YOU, YOU *SHOULD* BE ATTACKING THOSE WHO STRIKE OUT AT YOU!

YOU HAD THIS ALL FIGURED OUT, DIDN'T YOU, Q?

YOU'RE PITTING TWO DISPARATE, SENTIENT LIFE-FORMS AGAINST EACH OTHER...MORE TESTS, OR JUST FOR LAUGHS THIS TIME?

WELL, I'VE USUALLY BEEN ABLE TO SOLVE THESE PROBLEMS WITH-OUT RESORTING TO VIOLENCE. AND IF WE *ARE* FORCED TO MAKE A STAND, I'LL DECIDE WHEN WE DO-- *NOT YOU!*

ALSO, FINALLY, WE ARE *NOT* YOUR FRIENDS!

JEAN-LUC, YOU CUT ME TO THE QUICK.

CAPTAIN, THERE HAS BEEN SOME MINOR DAMAGE TO THE SHIP'S LIVING QUARTERS...

...AND WE ARE STILL BEING FIRED UPON.

THE CIVILIANS! CAPTAIN PICARD TO SICK BAY.

STATUS OF COMMANDER RIKER AND THE REST OF AWAY TEAM?

RIKER, HAHN AND GIBSON ARE FINE, SAVE FOR MINOR BRUISES, CAPTAIN.

BUT I'M AFRAID LIEUTENANT YAR IS STILL NOT IN ANY CONDITION TO--

VERY WELL, THEN, DOCTOR CRUSHER--

--BOTH YOU AND COMMANDER RIKER ARE ORDERED TO THE BRIDGE.

OVER.

WORF, DATA AND LAFORGE... TO THE *BATTLE BRIDGE,* IMMEDIATELY!

I CANNOT CONTINUE EITHER CONFRONTATION WITH THE CIVILIANS IN DANGER!

GOOD THINKING, CAPTAIN...

14

...THOUGH DON'T YOU THINK YOU ARE MERELY STAVING OFF THE INEVITABLE?

YOU ARE SAVAGES... THEY ARE SAVAGES...

YOU HAVE TO DESTROY THEM FIRST!

BATTLE BRIDGE CREW TAKE YOUR POSTS...

I'LL MAKE SURE RIKER AND COMPANY HAVE MANNED THE HELM.

LISTEN TO ME, I'M TRYING TO HELP YOU!

YOU AND YOUR RIKER REFUSED MY OFFERS BEFORE... I WILL NOT ACCEPT ANOTH--

PICARD TO BRIDGE--

RIKER HERE, SIR.

DOCTOR CRUSHER AND CON AND OP TEAM B ARE WITH ME, BUT WHAT EXACTLY HAS BEEN HAPPENING, SIR?

YOU WOULDN'T BELIEVE ME IF I TOLD YOU ANYWAY. SUFFICE IT TO SAY, THE SITUATION IS DICTATING DRASTIC MEASURES!

NO TIME TO GIVE FULL DETAILS, YET, COMMANDER--

AND THE NON-COMMISSIONED PASSENGERS ARE OUR PRIMARY CONCERN AT THE MOMENT!

AND THEY ARE HEREBY ORDERED TO THEIR QUARTERS UNTIL FURTHER NOTICE...

15

ALL DECKS ACKNOWLEDGING, SIR. STARSHIP SEPARATION... SIX, FIVE, FOUR, THREE, TWO, ONE...

DISENGAGE STAR DRIVE AND SAUCER SECTIONS OF THE ENTERPRISE!

COMMANDER... BEGIN COUNT-DOWN.

VOOOOSH

SHIP'S LOG, EXACT MOMENT OF SEPARATION, STAR-DATE 42127.8...

DATA, LAFORGE, FIRE PHOTON TORPEDOES THE MINUTE THE SAUCER IS SAFELY OUT OF THEIR RANGE!

PHOTONS AT THE READY, SIR.

FINALLY... SHOWING SOME OF YOUR TRUE COLORS, JEAN-LUC!

EXCELLENT! EXCELLENT!

16

WESLEY...CAN'T YOU SEE I'M--

BUT, MOM... I JUST SAW THE WEIRDEST THING, AND I KNOW I'M SUPPOSED TO STAY IN MY QUARTERS, BUT...

IT REALLY LOOKED TO ME LIKE THE ENTERPRISE'S BEEN BOARDED SOMEHOW! I'VE GOT TO TELL COMMAN--

WESLEY! NOT RIGHT NOW... TASHA'S STILL--

TASHA, NO!

NO!

NO!

HE'S HERE!

HE'S FOUND ME!

NO!

TASHA--?

DEANNA--?

ARE YOU OKAY?

NO... I...

HE'S HERE! I FEEL HIM... HE'S COME FOR TASHA! SHE'S...

NO!

DEANNA... WHAT IS IT?

NO!

HELM DOES NOT RESPOND!

SOMETHING'S VERY WRONG HERE, SIR!

COMMANDER...

WE'RE VEERING OFF OUR PLOTTED COURSE!

18

86

AWAITING FURTHER COMMANDS, CAPTAIN.

HOLD ANY ADDITIONAL FIRE, GEORDI.

STATUS, DATA?

SENSORS INDICATE THE ALIEN VESSEL IS MOST ASSUREDLY *DISABLED*.

ODD. ONE SHOT AND THEY'RE STOPPED COLD?

DON'T JUST STAND THERE, CAPTAIN...ORDER YOUR MEN TO OBLITERATE THE ENEMY!

BACK OFF, Q.

YOUR DESPERATION IS BEGINNING TO *SHOW THROUGH* ALL YOUR POMPOSITY AND POSTURING.

ONE MIGHT EVEN GET THE FEELING THAT ALL OF THIS SAVAGERY YOU'RE SO ANXIOUS TO ATTRIBUTE TO THE FEDERATION IS MERELY A PROJECTION OF YOUR OWN INSECURITY.

HUMAN DOUBLE-TALK AND *LIES*!

ARRRRRR!

FINALLY:...SHOWING SOME OF YOUR TRUE COLORS, Q!

EXCELLENT! EXCELLENT!

DON'T MOCK ME, PICARD—

19

--I COULD *SQUASH* YOU LIKE A--

THEN *DO IT!*

I'M *FED UP* WITH ALL YOUR *TESTS* AND *GAMES* AND *DECEPTION!*

CAPTAIN...

I'M RECEIVING A COMMUNIQUE... FROM THE ALIEN VESSEL.

WIPE ME OUT!

WIPE *THEM* OUT!

AND THEN BE ON YOUR MERRY WAY, TELLING YOURSELF YOU'RE *NOT GUILTY* OF EXACTLY WHAT YOU'RE ACCUSING US OF!

AT LEAST THEN I WON'T HAVE TO HEAR YOUR LINE OF BULL ANYMORE!

PUT IT UP, WORF...

QUICKLY, BEFORE Q GIVES IN TO HIS BASER URGES AND ACTUALLY CARRIES OUT HIS THREATS!

PLEASE... NO MORE SHOOTING...

AYE, SIR.

WE *DID NOT* WANT TO *FIGHT* ANYONE! WE WERE TOLD WE WOULDN'T HAVE TO FIGHT!

WE DO NOT KNOW HOW TO RUN THIS SHIP... IT'S COMPLETELY ALIEN TO US! WE CANNOT *DEFEND* OURSELVES!

ARE THOSE GUYS *HUMANS?*

ALL THIS TIME WE'VE BEEN UP AGAINST *US?!*

MOST INTRIGUING.

BECAUSE *OUR LEADER* HAS *ABAN-DONED* US!

HELP US... PLEASE!

SURELY YOU ARE NOT *BELIEVING* THEIR WORDS?

OBVIOUSLY *THEY* ARE HOSTILE HUMANS!

YOU *ARE* GOING TO DEAL WITH THEM ACCORD-INGLY...?

AREN'T YOU, CAPTAIN PICARD?

YES, IT'S ALL VERY CLEAR TO ME, NOW...

IT STRUCK ME AS UNUSUAL THAT WE WERE ABLE TO HALT THESE "ALIENS" SO EASILY EITHER...

WHY *HADN'T* THEY USED EVEN THE MOST RUDIMENTARY OF SHIELDING TO DEFEND THEMSELVES?

HINDSIGHT SHOWS THAT THEY WERE AS UNFAMILIAR WITH THE ALIEN VESSEL'S DESIGN AS WE WERE.

NOW I'M NOT EVEN SURPRISED THAT THERE ARE HUMANS OVER THERE! NOT WITH Q AND HIS FIXATION ON HUMANITY INVOLVED IN ALL OF THIS.

20

QUIET!

ALL RIGHT, Q... ANYTHING ELSE YOU'D LIKE ME TO DO?

YES...

DO SOMETHING *AGGRESSIVE!*

DESTROY THEM!

I'M AFRAID I *CANNOT* DO THAT, Q. IT'S AGAINST OUR RULES. BUT I WILL SHOW YOU WHAT I *CAN* DO.

DATA...

HAVE ENGINEERING LOCK ONTO THEIR COORDINATES AND BEAM THEM ABOARD THE ENTERPRISE.

EXACTLY HOW MANY PEOPLE ARE ON THAT SHIP?

MY READINGS SAY ONLY FOUR, SIR.

ONCE ON BOARD HAVE THEM BROUGHT HERE BEFORE ME.

NO!

I DO NOT WANT THEM HERE!

KILL THEM! *KILL THEM!*

I'M STILL CAPTAIN OF THE ENTERPRISE, Q...

...UNLESS YOU WANT TO SIMPLY TAKE HER AWAY FROM ME?

TAKE HER FROM YOU...?

YOU KNOW I... I CANNOT DO THAT!

IT'S AGAINST *THEIR* RULES!

I CAN *USE* YOU HUMANS TO ILLUSTRATE MY POINTS TO THEM...

BUT I... I CANNOT COMMIT SUCH AN ACT OF AGGRESSION MYSELF... IF THEY HAPPENED TO BE WATCHING...

THEY BEING YOUR PEOPLE? AS I THOUGHT, EVEN WITH ALL YOUR POWER, YOU ARE POWERLESS. YOU HAVE PRESENTED YOURSELF TO US AS SOME SORT OF *JUDGE* IN THE PAST, Q...

IS IT THAT YOU ARE THE ONE WHO IS BEING JUDGED ON THIS OCCASION?

CAPTAIN...

THE CREW OF THE ENEMY VESSEL.

LOOKS MORE LIKE YOU WERE HELPING *THEM!*

STATE YOUR NAMES AND YOUR PLACE OF ORIGIN.

YOU TOLD US THAT IF WE DID AS YOU SAID, WE WOULD BE RICH-- RESPECTED...

INSTEAD YOU DID NOTHING FOR US!

THERE HE IS!

Q, YOU PROMISED US WE WOULD STAND TRIUMPHANT!

21

89

90

CAPTAIN'S LOG; STARDATE 42128.3:

HAVING SUCCESSFULLY DISABLED THE AGGRESSIVE ALIEN VESSEL BEFORE US, WE HAVE TAKEN HER SURPRISINGLY *HUMAN* CREW ABOARD THE U.S.S. ENTERPRISE.

WHILE UNDER ATTACK BY THIS UNCLASSIFIED CARRIER, WE WERE FORCED TO JETTISON OUR CRAFT'S SAUCER SECTION.

USUALLY A SIMPLE STANDARD SAFETY PROCEDURE, DESIGNED TO SPARE THE LIVES OF OUR CIVILIAN PASSENGERS...

...I'M AFRAID I MAY HAVE DOOMED EVERYONE ABOARD HER WHEN I GAVE THE ORDER TO INITIATE THE MANEUVER, IN THIS PARTICULAR INSTANCE.

THE SAUCER IS *GONE* FROM THIS PLANE, CAPTAIN PICARD!

AND EVEN *I* AM NOT SURE *HOW*--OR *WHERE* IT'S GONE!

I AM IN NO MOOD FOR YOUR OMNIPOTENT TRICKERY, *Q!*

I WANT MY PEOPLE RETURNED TO ME... *IMMEDIATELY!*

I AGREE, SIR... THIS Q ENTITY HAS LIED TO US EVERY CHANCE HE'S GOTTEN!

BUT, LIEUTENANT *WORF,* ISN'T IT POSSIBLE THAT SOMEONE OTHER THAN MYSELF *MIGHT* BE RESPONSIBLE JUST ONCE?

IT IS *NOT* LIKELY.

I KNOW... YOU SEIZED FOUR HUMAN BEINGS FROM THAT WARSHIP...

AND I HAPPEN TO KNOW THERE WERE *FIVE* HUMANS ON THAT VESSEL!

YES, THAT'S IT...THE SOLE PERSON LEFT OVER THERE *BEAMED* TO YOUR SAUCER, COMMANDEERED IT AND--

BULL!

YOU ARE JUST TRYING TO CLOUD THE FACTS! YOU ALWAYS SEEM TO KNOW SO MUCH ABOUT WHAT'S GOING ON...

THEN YOU KNOW THAT I, FOR ONE, HAVE HAD ENOUGH OF YOUR--

UNHAND ME, KLINGON.

6-3706

THAT WILL BE ALL, Q! I'VE STOOD BY AND WATCHED YOU GO THROUGH THE MOTIONS OF YOUR ACT LONG ENOUGH!

AREN'T YOU LISTENING? I HAD NOTHING TO DO WITH YOU LOSING YOUR PRECIOUS SAUCER! AND IF YOU'RE SO FED UP WITH MY "ACT", WHY DON'T YOU DO SOMETHING ABOUT IT, CAPTAIN...SIR?

YOU'VE COME TO THE ENTERPRISE ONE TIME TOO MANY WITH YOUR INFERNAL TESTS AND JUDGMENTS ON US!

NOW YOU'VE HIDDEN HUNDREDS OF PEOPLE IN MY CHARGE AND YOU'VE INJURED THE LAST OF MY CREWMEN!

FIRST OFF...YOU'LL LOOK AT ME WHEN I'M ADDRESSING YOU ABOARD MY VESSEL, Q!

PICARD--? YOU DARE...?!

SIR.

I'M TELLING YOU, THEY HAVE YOUR SAUCER!

THEY WHO? AND WHERE?

I--I DON'T KNOW...I WASN'T INCLUDED...I--

I DO NOT HAVE TO ANSWER YOUR QUESTIONS, PICARD! I AM OF THE Q!

SIR, BACK OFF--HE'S ALREADY DECAPACITATED WORF...

AND WE KNOW HE CAN DO WORSE!

THEN LET HIM-- I HAVE NOTHING TO LOSE AT THIS POINT-- I'VE ALREADY LOST EVERYTHING!

YOU HAVE PLENTY TO LOSE PICARD, AND YOU SHALL, FOR PRESUMING TO SOIL A Q'S PERSONAGE WITH YOUR ANTAGONISTIC HUMAN TOUCH!

I, TOO, AM FED UP, AND YOU LEAVE ME WITH ONLY ONE COURSE-- TO ERADICATE YOU AND YOUR VALUED ENTERPRISE FROM EXISTENCE!

IN EFFECT SPARING OTHERS FROM THE SAME BOTHER I'VE HAD WITH YOU.

3

STAR TREK
THE NEXT GENERATION

COMMANDER'S LOG: STARDATE 42128.3:

AS ACTING CAPTAIN OF THE ENTERPRISE'S SAUCER SECTION, IT IS MY DUTY TO KEEP DETAILED ACCOUNTS OF OUR SITUATION AND ENTER THEM IN THIS LOG...

UNFORTUNATELY, ALL SHIP'S MONITORS AND INSTRUMENTATION ARE MALFUNCTIONING...

THE ENTERPRISE'S HULL IS ALSO VIBRATING TO DANGEROUSLY ALARMING DEGREES-- AND PANIC IS GRIPPING THE ENTIRE SAUCER AS WE PASS THROUGH SOME STRANGE NEW-- FOR LACK OF A BETTER TERM-- ANTI-SPACE.

MY FRUSTRATION: I DO NOT KNOW EXACTLY WHERE WE ARE-- OR WHERE WE ARE GOING.

Q's DAY

NCC-1701-D

4

MIKE CARLIN WRITER • PABLO MARCOS PENCILLER • CARLOS GARZON & ARNE STARR INKERS • BOB PINAHA LETTERER • CARL GAFFORD COLORIST • ROBERT GREENBERGER EDITOR

COMMANDER RIKER, MY CONSOLE'S *STILL* NOT RESPONDING!

I THINK IT'S SAFE TO SAY THE SAUCER'S COMPLETELY OUT OF OUR CONTROL AT THIS POINT, LT. BICKLEY.

COUNSELOR TROI, USING YOUR BETAZOID "GIFTS"--

--CAN YOU SENSE *ANYTHING* THAT MIGHT EXPLAIN WHAT'S HAPPENING TO US?

I--I'VE BEEN TRYING, SIR.

SINCE THIS BEGAN, I *HAVE* BEEN AWARE OF A PRESENCE-- BOTH FAMILIAR *AND* ALIEN TO ME.

COMMANDER, IT IS NO ONE AND EVERYONE!

FAT LOT OF GOOD INFO LIKE THAT'S GOING TO DO US, COMMANDER!

MAYBE ARGYLE IN ENGINEERING CAN--

YOU'RE OUT OF LINE, LT.

AND YOU ARE NOT HELPING MATTERS HERE, MISTER BICKLEY.

PERHAPS IF YOU STAY WITH YOUR MONITORS WHILE I STAY WITH *MINE,* WE CAN SOON SOLVE THIS PUZZLE TOGETHER.

AYE, SIR.

TROI, STAY WITH THAT PRESENCE...

I'LL CHECK ON HOW THE REST OF US ARE COPING WITH THIS MYSTERIOUS TAKE-OVER.

RIKER TO ALL STATIONS-- REPORT.

5

ENSIGN MILZOFF IN CORRIDOR 3K, SIR...

FOOTING IS SHAKY...

BUT EVERYONE'S COOPERATING AND GOING TO THEIR QUARTERS AS ORDERED.

THERE *IS* SOME CONCERN AMONG THE LAY PEOPLE...BUT WE'RE HANDLING IT, SIR.

EASY, MS. STRUTT...

BUT, MY HUSBAND-- HE'S ON THE OTHER SECTION--ARE THEY STILL IN *BATTLE?*

CAN WE CONTACT THEM? WHERE ARE *WE?*

AND WHY ARE WE *SHAKING* SO MUCH?

AS SOON AS WE KNOW, YOU'LL KNOW, MA'AM.

PLEASE DO NOT WORRY.

DOCTOR CRUSHER, COMMANDER...

I'M HEADING TO SICK BAY. THEY COULD PROBABLY USE MY HELP DURING THIS UNUSUAL DISTURBANCE.

MA...?

I THINK THIS RATTLING IS VERY SIMILIAR TO THE TURBULANCE A SHIP MIGHT THEORETICALLY EXPERIENCE TRANSVERSING DIMENSIONAL BRIDGES OR HYPER-SPACE. MAYBE COMMANDER RIKER WOULD LIKE ME TO--

JUST SIT TIGHT, WESLEY.

I'LL BE BACK AS SOON AS I'M SURE EVERYTHING'S ALL RIGHT.

I CAN SIT JUST AS TIGHT AT RIKER'S SIDE ON THE BRIDGE.

I KNOW I CAN BE OF SOME ASSISTANCE!

NURSE...NURSE... WHAT'S HAPPENING?

MY BED'S *MOVING!*

YES, I KNOW, MRS. FENAL-- *EVERYTHING'S* MOVING!

BUT YOU MUST LIE DOWN! YOU, TOO, MS. RAAZA!

BUT I DON'T FEEL VERY... WELL!

PLEASE, DON'T! EVERYTHING WILL BE ALL RIGHT!

LET'S JUST ALL RELAX-- LIKE LITTLE FENTON, HERE.

HE KNOWS THERE'S REALLY NOTHING TO WORRY ABOUT. RIGHT, FENTON?

UH-HUH. I--

UUUUUURRRR... HE'S *HERE*...HE'S COME FOR *ME*...

NURSE WILLIAM-- IT'S LT. YAR!

HE STALKED ME...ON THAT ALIEN SHIP...*

...HE FOLLOWED ME... FROM MY *COLONY*...

*LAST ISSUE.

...I MUST *FIGHT* HIM... CANNOT LET PAST REPEAT... MAY HURT OTHERS... I MUST--

HER SEDATIVE'S WORN OFF...IT'S A LITTLE EARLY FOR ANOTHER DOSE, BUT...

--STOP HIM...HE'S NEAR... I FEEL HIM... CANNOT JUST SIT HERE...

SETTLE DOWN, TASHA--

BE RIGHT BACK, FENTON... HANG TOUGH.

OKAY, MISTER WILLIAM.

--I'M COMING WITH SOME MORE REST AND RELAXATION, JUST AS THE DOCTOR ORD--

WHOA!

TRIPPED OVER SOME--

--THING!

PLA-THUNK- SHHH

⑦

HEY, IS THAT A--

CLOAKING DEVICE? YES. *MY* CLOAKING DEVICE.

AND YOU'VE SEEN TOO MUCH.

BOK!!

OOOF!

NURSE--?

TASHA? IT'S ME, *REGLECH,* DEAR--

--I'M *HOME!*

NO...

HALLUCINATING... MUST BE *SEDA-TIVES...*

ΞUGHFF... CAN'T MOVE...

TOO DISORIENTED...

IT HAS BEEN A LONG TIME, HASN'T IT, TASHA?

I'M TRAPPED... CAN'T MOVE...

JUST LIKE *THEN...* ON THE *COLONY...*

YOU...YOU...

THOSE *WERE* GOOD TIMES, EH, TASHA?

CARE TO *REMINISCE* WITH ME?

NOOOOOO!

8

PREPARE YOURSELF, PICARD...

YOU HAVE ANGERED ME *GREATLY!*

THE FEELING IS MUTUAL, Q.

SO CARRY OUT YOUR THREATS, AND *SPARE ME* ANY FURTHER AGGRAVATION.

OH, HO--VERY *BRAVE* SOUNDING, CAPTAIN MARTYR!

STILL *TALKING,* EH, Q?

WOULD IT BE EASIER FOR YOU TO DO ME IN IF I TURNED MY BACK TO YOU?

LIKE LIEUTENANT WORF OVER THERE DID?

NO, PICARD, IT WILL BE MORE *PLEASURABLE* FOR ME TO *SEE* YOUR EXPRESSION--

--AS YOU *DIE!*

I CAN'T BEAR TO WATCH!

IT IS ALL WE *CAN* DO, GEORDI...

WE ARE *HELPLESS* AGAINST POWER AS *VAST* AS Q'S!

NOW...

...AS I WAS *SAYING,* Q.

CAPTAIN PICARD! YOU'RE *OKAY?!* DATA, *LOOK!*

I SEE, GEORDI! AND I AM *PLEASED* AS WELL.

NOTHING.

NOTHING HAPPENED.

YOU SHOULD BE... YOU SHOULD HAVE BEEN *OBLITERATED!*

SORRY, Q... OBVIOUSLY REPORTS OF MY OBLITERATION HAVE BEEN GREATLY EXAGGERATED.

CAPTAIN--?

BUT... MY POWER...YOU CANNOT HAVE--

WHERE IS HE?

WORF! YOU'RE--

LET ME AT Q!

WELCOME BACK, LIEUTENANT WORF... NOW BACK OFF! THAT'S AN ORDER! IT WOULD APPEAR, Q, THAT ALL YOU CAN DO-- AND HAVE DONE-- IS BEING UNDONE!

NO! THIS CANNOT BE! I AM Q! I AM ALL!

STAY BACK, PICARD! ALL OF YOU! LEAVE ME BE...I MUST HAVE TIME... GET AWAY!

I SA!D-- --LEAVE-- --ME-- --ALONE!

I SUSPECT THAT'S EXACTLY WHAT'S HAPPENED, Q!

YOU REALLY HAVE BEEN REDUCED TO OUR LEVEL, EH, Q?

SWISH

WELL, GOOD!

CRAKK

BECAUSE I'VE BEEN DYING TO DO THAT SINCE I MET YOU!

BUT THEN YOU ALWAYS SAID WE HUMANS HAD THAT VIOLENCE IN US!

10

COMMANDER, I'M IN THE SICK BAY... AND I HATE TO *ADD* TO YOUR LIST OF TROUBLES, BUT...

THERE APPEARS TO HAVE BEEN SOME KIND OF *DISTURBANCE* DOWN HERE.

AND *NOT* JUST FROM ALL THE VIBRATING THE SHIP'S BEEN DOING.

COMMANDER, TASHA YAR IS *GONE!*

SIR, SHE WAS DELIRIOUS--RANTING AND RAVING--

--AND THE NIGHT NURSE WAS FOUND HERE... *UNCONSCIOUS.*

I SEE, DOCTOR CRUSHER...YOU WERE RIGHT, I DIDN'T NEED ANY PROBLEMS LIKE THAT.

I'LL GET SECURITY ON IT.

WILLIAM, I AM *CONCERNED.*

ME TOO, DEANNA. ME TOO.

THOUGHT MOM FOUND OUT I WAS GONE.

BUT TASHA'S MISSING--IN A WAY, I WISH SHE *HAD* FOUND ME OUT INSTEAD!

SECURITY, COMMANDER RIKER HERE...YOUR CHIEF, TASHA YAR'S TURNED UP *MISSING...* COMB THE ENTIRE SAUCER FOR HER! PRONTO!

AYE, SIR.

FINDING TASHA SHOULD BE *EASY--*

--COMPARED WITH THE LUCK WE'RE HAVING FIGURING OUT EXACTLY WHERE THIS WHOLE SHIP--

EH?

Q?!

QS COMMANDER.

AND *THEY* ARE WHAT HAD ME CONCERNED...

THEY ARE *WHERE* WE ARE!

OH, GOOD... VERY *GOOD.*

12

"DIDN'T I FOLLOW YOU *EVERY-WHERE?*

"WASN'T I THE ONLY ONE THERE FOR YOU IN THE ALLEYS AND GUTTERS OF THE COLONY?

"AND HOW DID YOU REPAY ME FOR ALL THAT *ATTENTION* I SHOWERED UPON YOU?

"YOU KEPT SCREAMING!

"YOU KEPT RIGHT ON SCREAMING-- UNTIL YOU *LEFT* THE COLONY!"

AND, *FINALLY,* AFTER ALL THESE YEARS--

FATE... OR Q, OR WHATEVER IT'S CALLED... HAS BROUGHT US TOGETHER!

PLEASE...

AND I CAN TRY TO SHOW YOU AGAIN HOW *DEEPLY* I CARE FOR YOU!

NO...

NEVER AGAIN!

WHOOMF!

OH, GOD...

GOD...

104

HURT, REGLECH?

REMEMBER HOW MUCH IT HURT *ME*, BACK ON THE COLONY?

URRRRR

YOU DIDN'T STOP THEN EITHER, DID YOU?

HEY...

AND, NO, YOU *WEREN'T* THE *ONLY* ONE, REGLECH... YOU ALL FORCED ME TO DO THINGS I DIDN'T WANT TO DO!

YOU ALL MADE ME *HATE* WHAT I WAS--YOU ALL MADE ME *RUN!*

NOW...IT'S MY TURN TO MAKE YOU *HURT!*

HEY...YOU TWO...PLEASE... GET HER...OFF OF ME...

SORRY.

WE CANNOT.

PHA...NOBODY HELPED YOU THEN EITHER, EH, YAR!

I SHOULD'VE *KILLED* YOU THEN...

NOW YOU HAD BETTER KILL *ME*...

BECAUSE...IF YOU DON'T...I FOUND YOU ONCE...I...I CAN FIND YOU AGAIN!

NOT A BAD IDEA, REGLECH--

15.

--AND IF I WAS YOU, I MIGHT DO IT.

BUT... IN CASE YOU HADN'T NOTICED... I AM NOT YOU.

I AM A FEDERATION OFFICER, NOW.

AND REGARDLESS OF WHAT I WAS TO YOU THEN--

--YOU ARE UNDER FEDERATION ARREST.

ARE YOU THINKING WHAT I'M THINKING?

OF COURSE... VERY PROMISING, INDEED.

COMMANDER... THEY'RE ALL SMILING?!

YES, NOT AT ALL LIKE THE Q WE KNOW.

STILL, BE CAREFUL...

I'VE HAD A TASTE OF THEIR POWER--

--AND IF THEY MISUNDERSTAND ANYTHING WE DO OR SAY...

--ONE OF THEM COULD WIPE US OUT WITH A THOUGHT...

16

...I'D HATE TO THINK WHAT *FOUR* OF THEM COULD DO TO US.

COMMANDER, I'M SUDDENLY SENSING--

COMMANDER...I'VE APPREHENDED THE PERSON RESPONSIBLE FOR--

TASHA, YOU'RE OKAY!

COMMANDER, WHO ARE ALL THESE *PEOPLE?*

THEY *ALL* LOOK LIKE Q!

WAIT...I REMEMBER NOW...HE WAS ON BOARD THE ENTERPRISE WHEN ALL THIS STARTED...

I'M AFRAID I'M STILL A LITTLE GROGGY, SIR...

I CAN "FEEL" THAT YOU ARE NOT FRIGHTENED BY THESE MULTIPLE QS, TASHA...

IT IS UNUSUAL THAT THEY HAVE MERELY PUT US ALL ON OUR GUARDS--

--AND NOT ON THE DEFENSIVE LIKE THE Q WE'VE ENCOUNTERED BEFORE.

TASHA, YOU ENTERED THE BRIDGE WITH *TWO* OF THESE BEINGS, DIDN'T YOU?

I WAS WRAPPED UP IN MY OWN LITTLE BATTLE, SIR, I GUESS, I--

PLEASE YAR, DO NOT FEEL REGRETS.

WE Q DID NOT BRING YOUR PLACE TO US FOR YOU TO ACT *UNNATURALLY.*

WE REGRET THAT OUR *TAINTED* SELF HAS REPEATEDLY VENTURED TO *YOUR* PLACE...AND THAT YOUR PLACE WAS NOT *READY* FOR THE CONCEPT OF A Q.

BUT YAR--ACTING UNAWARE OF OUR VIEWING--HAS HELPED CONVINCE US THAT YOUR HUMANITY IS INDEED PROGRESSING IN A FAVORABLE DIRECTION.

GOODNESS DOES OUTWEIGH BADNESS IN YOUR MAKEUP--*CONTRARY* TO WHAT OUR TAINTED SELF HAS REPORTED.

WE'RE SATISFIED, AS WELL, THAT THE Q WAS UNSUCCESSFUL IN *REGRESSING* TO YOUR PLACE WHEN HE TRANSVERSED THERE...

...RENDERING HIMSELF A POOR EXAMPLE OF WHAT OUR IMPRESSION OF HUMANITY IS, NOW THAT YOU'VE BEEN WITH US.

17

AND MY PHASER BELONGS TO *ME*, Q!

ARRRGHFFF!

YOU CANNOT DO THIS TO ME-- *I AM Q!*

FROM WHAT LITTLE I'M GETTING HERE--YOU *WERE* Q, MISTER!

NOW, GET UP AND HAND OVER THAT--

COMMANDER RIKER--

--TO STARDRIVE ENTERPRISE. COME IN, ENTERPRISE.

IT'S THE SAUCER!

THEY'RE *BACK!*

COMMANDER...

...REPORT ON YOUR WHEREABOUTS UNTIL NOW.

CAPTAIN, IT SOUNDS ODD, BUT WE'VE BEEN *WITHIN* THE Q--*INSIDE* THEIR COLLECTIVE CONSCIOUSNESS.

NO! THEY WOULD NOT HAVE *YOU* INSTEAD OF ME! I AM THEIRS!

SILENCE, Q-- CONTINUE RIKER...

WELL, SIR, AS YOU KNOW FROM THE LAST TIME, THERE IS MORE THAN ONE Q ENTITY.

YES, COMMANDER-- YOU WERE NEARLY ONE WITH THEM, AS I RECALL.

AYE, SIR... WELL, SOMEHOW TASHA'S INNER-RESOLVE HAS CONVINCED THE Q THAT HUMANITY--WHILE NOT NEARLY AS PERFECT AS THEY -- IS ON THE RIGHT TRACK.

AND THAT THE Q THEY'VE SENT AMONGST US HAS BEEN "TAINTED" BY HIS FREQUENT VISITS-- SERVING TO MAKE *THEM* LESS THAN PERFECT!

BOTTOM LINE, CAPTAIN, AS NEAR AS I CAN FIGURE IT, IS THAT THE Q WITH YOU IS *NOT* WITH THEM ANY LONGER... HE'S *OURS* FOR GOOD!

NO.

NO!

19

THEY CANNOT *ABANDON* ME!

I WILL NOT STAND FOR THIS!

I AM Q!

I'VE HAD IT ALL!

WORF--LOOK OUT! HE'S *STILL* GOT MY PHASER!

AND WITH IT, YOU STILL COWER BEFORE MY EVERY WHIM! THAT IS AS IT SHOULD BE!

FOR WITH YOUR PATHETIC WEAPON IN MY HAND, I CAN STILL *CONTROL* LIFE AND DEATH!

I WILL NOT BEAR BEING *HUMAN!*

I HAVE KNOWN *BETTER!*

AND IF I AM TO BE *REDUCED* TO YOUR LEVEL--

--I WOULD RATHER BE DEA--

STOP, Q, YOU FOOL!

PICARD--! CAN'T YOU LET ME EVEN--

OOOOOF!

BEEDEEDEEDEE

Q--THE PHASER--

20

HEY! WATCH WHERE YOU--

ARRRRR!

BEE DEE DEE DEOW

LAFORGE--?

LIEUTENANT--?

GEORDI--?!

NO!

YOU'VE *KILLED* GEORDI!

HE WAS NOT TO *BLAME* FOR WHAT'S BEFALLEN YOU--

--MURDERER!

GEORDI IS INNOCENT!

ACHHHH!

IT'S NOT *FAIR!*

DATA... EASY...

THIS IS NOT THE WAY...

...YOU TOLD *ME* THAT BEFORE!

TELL *THAT* TO GEORDI, NOW, WORF...

TELL HIM THAT NOW...

CAPTAIN'S LOG: STARDATE 41753.3:

ON A FAIRLY ROUTINE MISSION TO DOCUMENT THE QUESTIONED EXISTENCE OF THE LEGENDARY PLANET *FALTOS* IN SECTOR 902--

--THE *ENTERPRISE* AND HER CREW ENCOUNTERED A RENEGADE STARSHIP *AND* THE OMNIPOTENT ENTITY Q.

AS A SAFETY PRECAUTION, THE *SAUCER SECTION* OF OUR SHIP--ALONG WITH NON-COMMISSIONED CIVILIAN PASSENGERS-- WAS JETISONED.

SUBSEQUENTLY, THE SAUCER WAS *LOST* IN SPACE FOR SEVERAL HOURS AND HAS SINCE--INEXPLICABLY-- RETURNED AND JOINED THE *STARDRIVE SECTION* OF THE ENTERPRISE.

SIMULTANEOUSLY--AND PERHAPS AS A DIRECT COROLLARY TO THE SAUCER'S RETURN--Q HAS DISCOVERED HIMSELF STRIPPED OF ANY AND ALL POWERS HE ONCE MIGHT HAVE POSSESSED.

DISTRAUGHT, Q ATTEMPTED SUICIDE. BUT, IN A STRUGGLE TO PREVENT SUCH AN ACTION, LIEUTENANT *J.G. GEORDI LAFORGE* HAS BEEN STRUCK DOWN BY PHASER FIRE MEANT TO DESTROY Q...

Q AFFECTS!

GEORDI...?

HE IS...

...LIFELESS.

G-3774

| MIKE CARLIN WRITER | PABLO MARCOS PENCILLER | CARLOS GARZON ARNE STARR INKERS | BOB PINAHA LETTERER | CARL GAFFORD COLORIST | ROBERT GREENBERGER EDITOR |

THIS IS *IMPOSSIBLE* TO ACCEPT...

MY FRIEND... ONE OF THE FEW TO TREAT ME AS IF I WERE LIKE HIM...

LET ME GO... THAT SHOT WAS MEANT FOR *ME!* I'M THE ONE THAT SHOULD BE *DEAD!*

Q?!

CAPTAIN... HOLD TIGHT... DATA LOOKS AS IF HE'S GOING TO--

MISTER WORF, DATA IS NOT PROGRAMMED TO--

YOU'VE TAKEN MY ONLY FRIEND AWAY!

UCHHHHHH!

DATA-- *NO!*

CAN'T HOLD--DATA'S STRENGTH... TOO GREAT...

BRING HIM *BACK!*

BRING *GEORDI* BACK!

CRACK

ARRRGH!

YOU CAN DO *ANYTHING,* Q!

I'M TELLING YOU TO *MAKE GEORDI LIVE AGAIN!*

WHACK

2

114

--PLEASE, SIR...

IF YOU'RE NOT GOING TO LET ANY OF THESE PEOPLE PUT ME OUT OF MY MISERY...

...I BEG YOU TO STOP THIS PAIN AND LET THE DOCTOR TREAT ME--

--AS YOU OFFERED EARLIER... PLEASE!

DON'T DO IT, SIR!

HE'S EARNED EVERY MINUTE OF HIS AGONY! HE MUST HAVE MADE MORE PEOPLE SUFFER WITH HIS ACTIONS THAN MOST OF HUMANITY MAKES IN CENTURIES OF EXISTENCE!

PERHAPS, WORF--

--BUT MAYBE Q FEELS HE HAD REASONS FOR HIS ACTIONS!

WELL, Q... WHY DID YOU TRY TO PIT US AGAINST THOSE HUMAN COLONISTS BY MAKING US THINK WE'D FACED HOSTILE ALIEN LIFE?

PLEASE... THE HURT...

AND WHY, SPECIFICALLY, PEOPLE WHO'D BEEN ASSOCIATED WITH OUR LIEUTENANT YAR?

I... WAS DESPERATE...

I HAD TO PROVE HOW WRONG HUMANITY WAS...

THE Q WERE GROWING MORE AND MORE INTERESTED IN HUMANITY SINCE IT STARTED REVEALING ITS TRUE POTENTIAL IN RECENT TIMES.

SO...

YOU FINALLY ADMIT THAT WE AREN'T AS BAD AS YOU'VE BEEN TRYING TO CONVINCE US WE ARE.

THAT IS WHAT YOU'RE SAYING, ISN'T IT?

7

OF COURSE YOU'RE NOT THAT BAD... OR THE Q WOULDN'T HAVE OFFERED *YOU* A PLACE WITH THEM!

AND THAT IS EXACTLY WHERE *I* HAVE FAILED!

CAN YOU EXPLAIN TO US WHAT *THAT* MEANS?

IT WAS MY *ASSIGNMENT*, COUNSELOR TROI, TO BRING HUMANITY INTO THE Q.

HUMANITY PASSED PRELIMINARY TESTS, I BROUGHT YOUR RIKER TO THEM.

BUT, AS YOU KNOW, HE DECLINED OUR GIFTS.

AND, SUBSEQUENTLY FAILING TO SUBMIT ANY SUITABLE HUMAN TO THE Q, *MY* POSITION WITH THEM GREW SHAKY!

AND YOU GREW MORE AND MORE DESPERATE.

BUT WHAT MADE YOU THINK YOUR ENCOUNTER WITH US THIS TIME WOULD'VE BEEN ANY DIFFERENT?

I TRIED TO COME HERE WITHOUT THE REST OF THE Q KNOWING...

BUT, AS I FEARED, *THAT* WAS IMPOSSIBLE.

I REALIZED THAT THE LAST TIME--WHEN RIKER TURNED US DOWN--THAT YOU ALL STOOD BY HIM AND HIS DECISION.

I THOUGHT THIS TIME I MIGHT BE ABLE TO INDUCT YOU *ALL* INTO THE Q.

THE *ENTIRE* ENTERPRISE CREW?

YES... YOUR VESSEL IS MANNED WITH THE FINEST HUMANITY HAS TO OFFER... AND I THOUGHT...

...I THOUGHT...

Q!

CAPTAIN... ALLOW ME...

EXCEPT, IT IS HIS CONTENTION THAT, WITH HIS EVERY VISIT TO US, HE WAS BECOMING MORE AND MORE HUMAN HIMSELF.

HENCE, HIS MAKING MORE AND MORE *MISTAKES* IN JUDGMENT.

HE'S STILL ALIVE... MERELY FAINTED... AND I CAN *SENSE* HE FEELS HE MIGHT HAVE SUCCEEDED IN BRINGING HUMANITY TO THE Q.

8

RIKER, TROI, PLEASE ESCORT Q TO THE SICK BAY.

AYE, SIR.

SIR, I WILL THEN FILE A REPORT ON WHAT HAPPENED TO THE SAUCER WHILE WE WERE GONE.

AYE, SIR.

VERY GOOD, NUMBER ONE...WE WILL RENDEZVOUS ON THE MAIN BRIDGE AT SIXTEEN HUNDRED HOURS.

IF I MAY BE SO BOLD, CAPTAIN...

I FIND IT HARD TO BELIEVE THAT WE'RE ACTUALLY GOING TO HELP Q AFTER ALL HE'S PUT US THROUGH, SIR.

HE IS NOT THE SAME BEING HE WAS BEFORE, LIEUTENANT.

HE'S CHANGED-- IN PROBABLY THE MOST ENCOMPASSING SENSE OF THE WORD.

AND WE'RE DIFFERENT NOW AS WELL, THANKS TO HIS PERSISTENT VISITS TO US.

SOME OF US ARE CHANGED AS PERMANENTLY AS HE MIGHT BE.

LIEUTENANT, WON'T YOU JOIN ME IN VACATING THE BATTLE BRIDGE?

AYE, SIR, BUT...

DO WE REALLY HAVE TO ACCEPT Q AMONGST US WITH SUCH OPENED ARMS?

WORF, I SEEM TO RECALL AN ENTIRE RACE OF FORMERLY MALEVOLENT BEINGS BEING WELCOMED INTO THE FEDERATION IN A SIMILAR FASHION NOT VERY LONG AGO.

YES...CAPTAIN... YOUR POINT IS CLEAR...

BUT IT IS THAT VERY KLINGON BACKGROUND THAT'S GOING TO MAKE IT HARD FOR ME TO LIKE THIS.

I AM NOT ASKING YOU TO LIKE IT, WORF--JUST LIVE WITH IT.

9

CAPTAIN'S LOG: SUPPLEMENTAL:

ACCORDING TO COMMANDER RIKER'S REPORT, NOT ALL Q ARE OUR ENEMY...

...AND THIS FAULTED MEMBER OF THEIR COLLECTIVE CONSCIOUSNESS HAD BEEN ABANDONED FOR HIS SHORTCOMINGS.

LIKE IT OR NOT, Q WAS ALL OURS NOW.

I DO NOT LIKE IT.

DATA...MOM SAYS THAT GEORDI IS NOT *GONE* YET.

HE'S CRITICAL... BUT HE *IS* HOLDING ON.

I AM PLEASED TO KNOW THAT, WESLEY...

WHAT I DO NOT LIKE IS, WHY YOUR MOTHER IS TENDING Q?

WHY IS SHE NOT WITH GEORDI... WHEN HE, ONE OF OUR OWN, IS SO CLOSE TO THE EDGE?

Q IS RAPIDLY NEARING DEATH, DATA...

AND THOUGH HIS CONDITION IS BAD, GEORDI IS *NOT* WORSENING.

AT THIS POINT, THERE IS LITTLE WE CAN ACTIVELY DO FOR GEORDI BESIDES PRAY.

THAT IS WHAT I HAVE BEEN DOING, WESLEY...

PRAYING TO GEORDI'S GOD...

BUT IT DOES NOT RELIEVE MY CONCERN.

IT'S STILL HARD TO BE *PLEASED* THAT THE CAPTAIN AND THE SHIP'S DOCTOR ARE ATTEMPTING TO AID THE ONE WHO DID THIS TO GEORDI.

ONE WHO HIMSELF PRAYS TO *BE* DEAD.

DATA...NO MATTER WHAT Q WAS BEFORE, HE IS A *MAN* NOW.

AND WE'VE ALL GOT TO DO WHATEVER WE CAN FOR OUR FELLOW MAN.

WE WOULD ALL WANT THE *SAME* DONE FOR *US*.

10

BUT Q WAS SO MALEVOLENT...

...HE WOULD NOT HAVE DONE THE SAME FOR US.

I'M AFRAID THAT THAT IS NOT FOR US TO JUDGE.

IT WAS PASSING JUDGMENTS ON OTHERS THAT HAS LED TO THIS SITUATION.

COUNSELOR...I KNOW I'VE ASKED YOU THIS A LOT TONIGHT, BUT--

OF COURSE, DATA, I UNDERSTAND...

I CAN SENSE, GEORDI...STILL WITH US... BARELY.

IN YOU, DATA... I CAN FEEL MUCH FEAR AND CONFUSION... AS WELL AS ANGER.

PERHAPS SOME TIME AWAY FROM THE SICK BAY WOULD DO *YOU* SOME GOOD.

AS YOU SAY, THERE IS NOTHING FOR YOU TO DO HERE.

I...I...

IT...IT MAKES ME MAD...

IN WAYS I AM THE ULTIMATE MAN... YET, HERE, I AM SO...HELPLESS...

COME ON, DATA...WHAT DO YOU SAY TO SOME HOLO-BALL?

BUT...

NO "BUTS"...DOCTOR'S SON'S ORDERS.

C'MON.

WELL, WILLIAM...DATA'S ALWAYS WANTED TO BE HUMAN--

--I GUESS THAT MEANS TAKING THE BAD WITH THE GOOD.

PERHAPS, DEANNA...

...BUT NOBODY DESERVES TO FEEL AS *CONFUSED* BY HIS EMOTIONS AS DATA IS.

11

THE DETENTION DECK!

THANKS TO YOU, REGLECH--

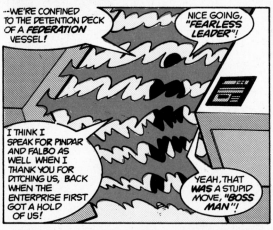

--WE'RE CONFINED TO THE DETENTION DECK OF A *FEDERATION* VESSEL!

NICE GOING, *"FEARLESS LEADER"!*

I THINK I SPEAK FOR PINDAR AND FALBO AS WELL WHEN I THANK YOU FOR DITCHING US, BACK WHEN THE ENTERPRISE FIRST GOT A HOLD OF US!

YEAH, THAT *WAS* A STUPID MOVE, *"BOSS MAN"!*

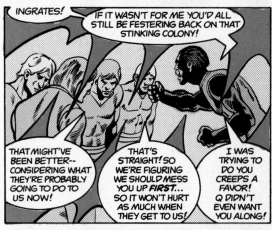

INGRATES!

IF IT WASN'T FOR ME YOU'D ALL STILL BE FESTERING BACK ON THAT STINKING COLONY!

THAT MIGHT'VE BEEN BETTER-- CONSIDERING WHAT THEY'RE PROBABLY GOING TO DO TO US NOW!

THAT'S STRAIGHT! SO WE'RE FIGURING WE SHOULD MESS YOU UP *FIRST*... SO IT WON'T HURT AS MUCH WHEN THEY GET TO US!

I WAS TRYING TO DO YOU CREEPS A FAVOR! Q DIDN'T EVEN WANT YOU ALONG!

AHHH, WHAT'S THE SENSE OF REASONING WITH *IDIOTS*?

BROCK

Q WAS RIGHT... THERE IS NO HOPE FOR TOADS LIKE YOU!

WHUD

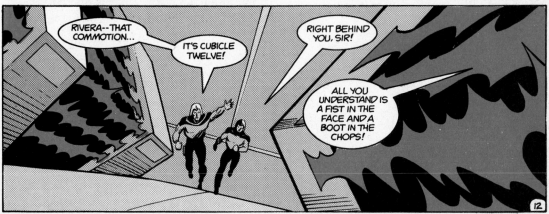

RIVERA-- THAT COMMOTION...

IT'S CUBICLE TWELVE!

RIGHT BEHIND YOU, SIR!

ALL YOU UNDERSTAND IS A FIST IN THE FACE AND A BOOT IN THE CHOPS!

12

--YOU'RE GOING RIGHT BACK DOWN AGAIN!

UHHHHNNN!

REGLECH...YOU REALLY HAD ME GOING THERE FOR A SECOND...

BEEDEEDEEDEE

...I WAS A LITTLE SURPRISED WHEN YOU USED *ME* AS A DIVERSION.

BUT, HEY, IT WORKED, EH!

SO WHERE DO WE GO FROM HERE, REGLECH?

AGAIN WITH THE "WE," PINDAR?

YOU REALLY DON'T GET THE HINT, DO YOU?

BEEDEE DEEDEE

GET *THIS*?

LEARNED ONE THING FROM BEING INVOLVED WITH Q...

...I'M BETTER OFF ON MY OWN.

SECURITY CHIEF YAR TO CAPTAIN PICARD.

COME IN, CAPTAIN PICARD.

15

WORF...WHERE IS THE CAPTAIN?

I'VE BEEN PAGING HIM UP AND DOWN THE SHIP.

HE'S IN HIS READY ROOM, TASHA...

AND HE'S LEFT EXPRESS ORDERS *NOT* TO BE DISTURBED.

FUNNY... GEORDI LAFORGE IS NOT THE FIRST MAN I'VE HAD TO WITNESS BEING CUT DOWN...

HE'S NOT EVEN THE FIRST I MIGHT'VE BEEN ABLE TO *SAVE* HAD I REACTED SLIGHTLY DIFFERENTLY.

I'M STILL TRYING TO JUSTIFY THAT EARLIER *INCIDENT* TO MYSELF...

...AND NOW *THIS*.

BY HANDLING Q LIKE I DID--AND LIKE I HAVE EVERY TIME WE'VE ENCOUNTERED HIM--I HAVE SPARED THE LIVES OF HUNDREDS...

AND I DEFINITELY KEPT Q FROM KILLING *HIMSELF* WITH MY ACTIONS...

...BUT THAT ONE STRAY PHASER-SHOT-- STRIKING GEORDI... I CANNOT HELP BUT FEEL THAT I WAS RESPONSIBLE.

THAT MY HANDS WERE ON THAT PHASER...

IF ONLY I HAD-- EH?

WHAT'S ALL THAT DIN?

LIEUTENANT WORF? WORF? A LITTLE QUIET, PLEASE!

DAMN!

16

A MOMENT'S PEACE IS PERHAPS TOO MUCH TO ASK FOR...

WHAT *IS* GOING ON OUT HERE?

SORRY, CAPTAIN PICARD--

--BUT I DID TRY TO KEEP THE LIEUTENANT FROM DISTURBING YOU.

LET ME GO, WORF... THIS IS AN *EMERGENCY!*

DON'T MAKE ME HAVE TO *MAKE* YOU LET ME GO!

THAT'LL BE QUITE ENOUGH OUT OF YOU TWO...

...THAT'S AN *ORDER!*

AYE, SIR.

AM I DEALING WITH THE BICKLEYS HERE?

SORRY, SIR.

EXPLANATION, LIEUTENANT.

REGLECH'S ESCAPED, SIR.

UNTIL YESTERDAY I MIGHT HAVE BEEN CONCERNED FOR MYSELF.

REGLECH REPRESENTED A PART OF MY LIFE THAT I'D FEARED MIGHT COME BACK TO HAUNT ME.

FACING UP TO HIM--I HAVE FACED UP TO MY DEEP IRRATIONAL FEARS.

IF HE COMES FOR ME THIS TIME, SIR, I KNOW I CAN HANDLE HIM.

BUT IF HE WERE TO GO FOR SOMEONE ELSE...

HMMMM... SOMEONE ELSE...

CAPTAIN...

WASN'T REGLECH INVOLVED IN A CONFRONTATION WITH Q EARLIER?

REGLECH *IS* DRIVEN BY FEELINGS OF REVENGE, SIR.

TASHA, COME WITH ME.

WORF, YOU HAVE THE CON.

AYE, SIR.

17

COMMANDER... COUNSELOR...

Q IS COMING TO...

WILL HE LIVE, DOCTOR CRUSHER?

UNFORTUNATELY FOR HIM... YES.

OOOOO... MY HEAD...

TAKE IT SLOWLY, Q... YOU'RE NOT ONE HUNDRED PERCENT YET BY ANY MEANS.

NOW, IF YOU NEED ME FOR ANY REASON--

--I'LL JUST BE A FEW METERS AWAY ADMINISTERING TO LIEUTENANT LAFORGE.

HURRY, PLEASE, DOCTOR...I'M NO EXPERT...BUT THESE READINGS...

DOCTOR, COULD ALL OF THE TIME YOU SPENT WITH Q HAVE COST GEORDI HIS LIFE?

DEANNA... Q WAS IN WORSE SHAPE...

THEN PERHAPS...BUT NOW THERE IS ABSOLUTELY *NOTHING* COMING FROM GEORDI.

NEITHER THROUGH YOUR INSTRUMENTS NOR THROUGH MYSELF!

"I AM CONCERNED THAT DEATH IS DRAWING NEARER."

18

NICE SHOT, DATA... BUT I ACED IT!

VERY IMPRESSIVE, WESLEY.

HEADS UP... IT'S COMING BACK AT YOU, DATA!

MY HEAD IS UP.

DATA... YOU MISSED!

THAT SHOT WAS A PIECE OF CAKE-- YOU'RE NOT EVEN TRYING!

INQUIRY: PIECE OF CAKE?

DON'T TRY TO CHANGE THE SUBJECT, DATA...

YOUR HEART'S NOT IN THIS IS IT?

WESLEY, GEORDI IS THE ONLY TRUE FRIEND I HAVE EVER HAD.

HE DOES NOT SEE ME FOR THE SYNTHETIC MAN I AM... HE SEES ME FOR WHO I AM.

IF I WERE TO LOSE GEORDI'S FRIENDSHIP... I...

I AGREE, DATA, THAT MORE PEOPLE SHOULD HAVE TO WEAR VISORS LIKE GEORDI'S.

IT REALLY SEEMS TO HELP HIM SEE PAST A LOT OF THINGS THE REST OF US HAVE HAD A HARD TIME GETTING OVER.

"COME ON, DATA, LET'S HEAD BACK TO SICK BAY AND SNEAK A PEEK AT YOUR BUDDY."

I ASSURE YOU...

I'VE DONE EVERYTHING HUMANLY POSSIBLE FOR GEORDI, DEANNA.

WE CAN ONLY WAIT AND WATCH.

Q!

WHO--?

19

OH...REGLECH...THEY'RE FINALLY GOING TO LET SOMEONE PUT ME OUT OF MY MISERY...

THANK YOU, KEGLECH.

QUIET, Q... OR THEY'LL--

Q?!

COMMANDER, WHAT IS...?

WE'RE LOSING Q AGAIN!

WILLIAM!

NO ONE'S STOPPING ME THIS TIME!

IF I'M GOING BACK TO THE COLONY, I'M GOING FOR A REASON!

BEEDEEDEEDEEOW

THIS PHASER'S SET ON KILL, SO DON'T--

HUH?

BEEDEEDEEDAK!

BACK AWAY FROM Q, REGLECH!

YOU HEARD THE CAPTAIN, SCUM... MOVE IT!

DAMN.

I CANNOT FATHOM THIS HUMANITY.

AFTER ALL I'VE PUT THEM THROUGH--

--THEY STILL GO TO SUCH GREAT LENGTHS TO KEEP ME WITH THEM.

WILLIAM, ARE YOU ALL RIGHT?

YES, DEANNA... FINE.

I'M BACKING, TASHA, DEAR, I'M BACKING...

LET'S GO, REGLECH...BACK IT UP!

20

131

LIEUTENANT YAR, I AM SENSING SOMETHING **WRONG** IN REGLECH...

HE IS GOING TO--

VERY PERCEPTIVE, BETAZOID...YOU'RE RIGHT ON THE MONEY!

--GO FOR GEORDI!

COUNSELOR... DOCTOR...

NO...

YOU'RE BLOCKING MY LINE OF FIRE!

I DOWNED TWO GUARDS EARLIER--

--AND THAT MEANS **TWO** PHASERS WERE MINE FOR THE TAKING!

NOW **YOU ALL** BACK OFF!

REGLECH...

THEIR ALLY LAFORGE IS... HELPLESS...

TAKE MY LIFE INSTEAD!

FORGET IT, Q... I TRIED YOU ALREADY! THESE HUMANS DON'T GIVE A DAMN ABOUT WHAT HAPPENS TO YOU!

DROP YOUR WEAPON, TASH!

NOW, THE BLIND MAN... HIM THEY CARE ABOUT! AND HE'S DEAD UNLESS I GET WHAT I WANT!

NO!

GEORDI'S BEEN THROUGH ENOUGH!

DATA... WAIT...

HOLD IT RIGHT THERE, TOUGH MAN!

OR **YOU'LL** BE MADE THE BAD EXAMPLE FOR THE OTHERS!

21

HA! I GOT WHO I CAME TO GET!

AS DID I... DROP IT, REGLECH.

ARR!

LET ME FINISH WRAPPING THIS UP, DATA.

THANK YOU... TASHA... I AM... TOO...RUN DOWN... TO HAVE GONE...ANY FURTHER...

THERE WAS NO WAY Q COULD HAVE SURVIVED SUCH AN ASSAULT-- IN HIS HUMAN STATE!

TO THINK HE WAS ONCE ONE OF THE MOST POWERFUL BEINGS IN OUR COSMOS.

NONSENSE. STILL AM! PUNY HUMAN PHASER-FIRE IS NOT ENOUGH TO ELIMINATE A Q!

Q?!

IMPOSSIBLE.

NOT REALLY, PICARD. THE COLLECTIVE Q TELLS ME I HAVE PASSED THEIR TEST.

MY SELFLESS ACT IN DATA'S DEFENSE HAS ALLOWED ME TO REJOIN THE Q. YOUR EXAMPLES TO ME HAVE FINALLY GIVEN THE Q HUMANITY--

--IT'S THE LEAST WE CAN DO TO RETURN THE FAVOR.

WHAT--WHAT'S HAPPENING?

GEORDI?!

CAPTAIN'S LOG; STARDATE 41753.9:

WITH LIEUTENANT LaFORGE MIRACULOUSLY RETURNED TO PERFECT HEALTH, AND REGLECH AND HIS SURVIVING COLONISTS HANDED OVER TO FEDERATION AUTHORITIES--

--THE ENTERPRISE EMBARKS ON ITS LONG DELAYED MAPPING MISSION, TO RECORD THE EXISTENCE OF THE ELUSIVE PLANET, FALTOS.

AND, AS RIDICULOUS AS THIS SOUNDS--

--I CANNOT HELP FEELING WE COULD'VE USED SOMEONE LIKE Q AT OUR SIDE ON THIS TREK.

CAPTAIN'S LOG: STARDATE 41753.8:

THE U.S.S. *ENTERPRISE* IS ON THE VERGE OF SPACE SECTOR 902...

...AND ON THE VERGE OF DOCUMENTING THE EXISTENCE OF THE LEGENDARY PLANET *FALTOS*.

OR *NOT*... IF IT IS INDEED A MYTHICAL PLACE SIMPLY CONJURED UP FOR ANCIENT FABLES AND FANCIFUL FAIRY TALES, AS SOME FEAR.

STEADY AS SHE GOES, LIEUTENANT *LAFORGE*.

IT HAD TAKEN OUR SHIP SEVERAL STANDARD MONTHS TO REACH THIS RIM OF CHARTED SPACE...

...AND IT WAS NOW ONLY A MATTER OF HOURS BEFORE WE'D KNOW WHETHER OR NOT THE FEDERATION HAD WASTED ITS TIME ON THIS MISSION.

AYE, SIR.

LIEUTENANT *DATA*... ENTER THE FOLLOWING COORDINATES:

194 MARK 4 AT WARP 6.3 ON MY MARK.

ACCORDING TO MOST ACCEPTED REPORTS THE FEDERATION'S RECEIVED-- *THAT* IS WHERE WE WILL FIND FALTOS.

BEGGING YOUR PARDON, CAPTAIN *PICARD*.

BUT I *CANNOT* ENTER THOSE COORDINATES.

DATA--?!

WHAT DO YOU MEAN YOU *CANNOT*, LIEUTENANT COMMANDER?

I HAVE GIVEN YOU AN *ORDER*.

WITH ALL DUE RESPECT, SIR, I CANNOT ENTER THE COORDINATES YOU'VE DICTATED...

BECAUSE, QUITE FRANKLY, THEY ARE *WRONG*.

G-378l

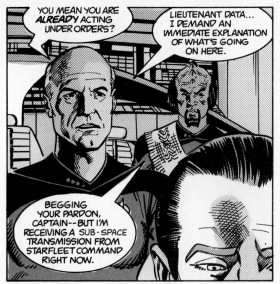

YOU MEAN YOU ARE *ALREADY* ACTING UNDER ORDERS?

LIEUTENANT DATA... I DEMAND AN IMMEDIATE EXPLANATION OF WHAT'S GOING ON HERE.

BEGGING YOUR PARDON, CAPTAIN--BUT I'M RECEIVING A SUB-SPACE TRANSMISSION FROM STARFLEET COMMAND RIGHT NOW.

RIGHT ON SCHEDULE.

TIKA TAK

TAK AKA TAK

YOU SHOULD BE ABLE TO GET THE EXPLANATION YOU DESIRE FROM THE HORSE'S MOUTH.

LIEUTENANT WORF... PUT STARFLEET ON THE SCREEN.

DATA, I AM YOUR FRIEND, RIGHT? DO YOU MIND IF I ASK YOU A PERSONAL QUESTION?

ARE YOU CRAZY? DO YOU WANT TO GET COURT-MARTIALED?

HARDLY. APPARENTLY THIS PARTICULAR PROGRAM INSIDE ME WASN'T SET TO BE ACTIVATED UNTIL WE REACHED 90Z. IN A WAY, I SUPPOSE I CANNOT HELP BUT DO WHAT I AM DOING.

CAPTAIN ≡SSSS≡ PICARD OF ≡SSSSS≡ THE U.S.S. ENTERPRISE ≡SSSSS≡

YES...ADMIRAL THIVOV...PLEASE EXCUSE THE POOR QUALITY OF OUR CONNECTION.

YOU ARE ≡SSSSS≡ FARTHER OUT THAN ANY COMMISSIONED VESSEL ≡SSSSS≡ HAS EVER BEEN BEFORE, CAPTAIN ≡SSSSS≡ IT IS TO BE EXPECTED.

TO BUSINESS, CAPTAIN...≡SSSSS≡ FROM THIS POINT FORWARD, YOUR ORDERS ≡SSSSS≡ ARE TO DO *ANYTHING* LIEUTENANT DATA INSTRUCTS.

I REALIZE THAT THESE ARE ≡SSSSS≡ UNUSUAL COMMANDS, CAPTAIN... BUT THE SUCCESS ≡SSSSS≡ OF MISSION: FALTOS RELIES ON ALL OF YOUR COOPERATION ≡SSSSS≡ ONE HUNDRED PERCENT.

ADMIRAL, THIS *IS* HIGHLY UNORTHODOX... BUT I MIGHT FIND IT EASIER TO PARTICIPATE TOWARD THE FEDERATION'S GOALS IF I WAS GIVEN FULL DETAILS OF--

THE ADMIRAL IS GROWING FAINTER, CAPTAIN.

I CAN SEE *AND* HEAR THAT, COUNSELOR TROI.

ADMIRAL PURCELL IS GONE, SIR.

DATA'S TAKEN US OUT OF COMMUNICATION RANGE.

LIEUTENANT, I'M CURIOUS...HAS STARFLEET BEEN AWARE OF HOW TO GET TO FALTOS ALL ALONG? IS THAT WHY *YOU* WERE ASSIGNED TO THE ENTERPRISE IN THE FIRST PLACE?

NO, SIR...NO HUMAN ALIVE KNOWS HOW TO GET TO FALTOS.

BUT *YOU* KNOW, DATA!

COMMANDER, IT IS COMMON KNOWLEDGE THAT I AM FAR FROM HUMAN.

THEN WHY DIDN'T YOU LOG THESE COORDINATES ALL ALONG?

I MYSELF WAS NOT AWARE I KNEW *HOW* UNTIL MOMENTS AGO, COUNSELOR.

HOW THEN DID YOU SUDDENLY COME UPON THIS KNOWLEDGE? WHO COULD HAVE PROGRAMMED THIS INTO YOU?

I CAN NEVER KNOW *EXACTLY* WHO HAS GIVEN ME A LOT OF WHAT I KNOW.

MAYBE I CAN HELP YOU...WITH MY BETAZOID BACKGROUND--

--PERHAPS I CAN ACCESS INFORMATION YOU CANNOT REACH.

YOU ARE FREE TO TRY, COUNSELOR...I HAVE NOTHING TO HIDE.

TAKA TIKA TAK

OOOOH...

SO...*COLD*...SO VAST INSIDE THE SYNTHETICS...

BUT I *CAN* SEE THE MANY HUMAN *MEMORIES* STORED WITHIN...

SO MANY LIVES...SO MUCH *INFORMATION*...THE STRONGEST...DOCTOR SOONG'S...

SOONG...HE IS THE MAN WHO *CREATED* ME.

IT'S SO *FAR*...ONLY CERTAIN STIMULI CAN TRIGGER SOME OF DATA'S MORE REMOTE ACCESS ABILITIES...

BUT THEN *HOW* DID THE FEDERATION KNOW THAT ENTERING 902 WOULD SET OFF DATA'S MEMORY BANKS?

WAIT, CAPTAIN--

--THERE IT IS. I'VE DONE IT.

WHERE? I DON'T SEE ANYTH--

4

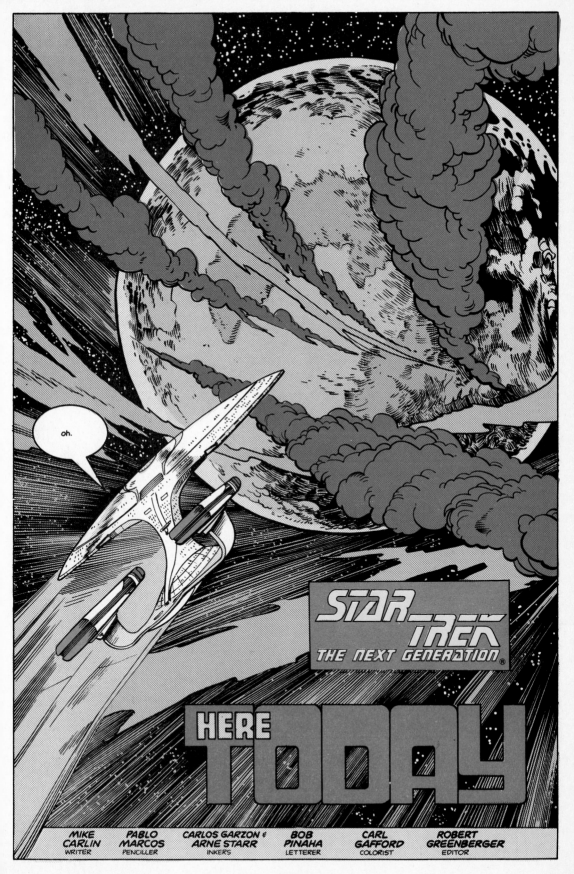

oh.

STAR TREK
THE NEXT GENERATION

HERE TODAY

MIKE CARLIN
WRITER

PABLO MARCOS
PENCILLER

CARLOS GARZON &
ARNE STARR
INKERS

BOB PINAHA
LETTERER

CARL GAFFORD
COLORIST

ROBERT GREENBERGER
EDITOR

FANNNNTASTIC.

GORGEOUS.

INTRIGUING.

FALTOS.

ONE OF THE TWELVE WONDERS OF THE UNIVERSE.

WORF--OPEN ALL HAILING FREQUENCIES.

FIND OUT IF THERE'S ANYONE DOWN THERE.

LAFORGE-- SCAN FALTOS-- GET AS MUCH FACTUAL INPUT INTO THE SHIP'S COMPUTER AS POSSIBLE...

THAT IS, OF COURSE, IF ALL THAT'S OKAY WITH MISTER DATA.

THOSE ORDERS WILL FACILITATE EXACTLY WHAT WE ARE SUPPOSED TO DO NEXT, SIR.

CAPTAIN, I'VE ESTABLISHED CONTACT WITH THE RESIDENTS OF FALTOS--

--AND THEY WELCOME US TO THEIR PLANET WITH OPEN ARMS.

MAY I ADD THAT I WOULD BE LEERY OF SUCH A TRANSPARENTLY FRIENDLY OVERTURE?

APPARENTLY KLINGONS ARE STILL LEERY OF ANYONE--

--WE IN THE FEDERATION, ON THE OTHER HAND, ARE NOT.

RIKER, ORGANIZE A DIPLOMATIC LANDING CREW.

YAR, WORF, TROI, LAFORGE AND--

YES, CAPTAIN PICARD--

--I AM GOING TOO.

6

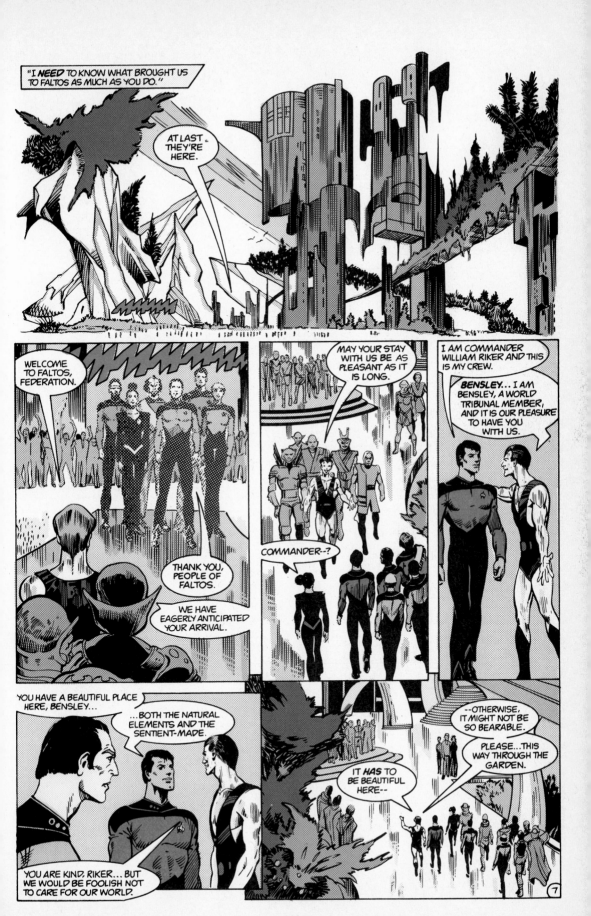

"I *NEED* TO KNOW WHAT BROUGHT US TO FALTOS AS MUCH AS YOU DO."

AT LAST, THEY'RE HERE.

WELCOME TO FALTOS, FEDERATION.

THANK YOU, PEOPLE OF FALTOS.

WE HAVE EAGERLY ANTICIPATED YOUR ARRIVAL.

MAY YOUR STAY WITH US BE AS PLEASANT AS IT IS LONG.

COMMANDER--?

I AM COMMANDER WILLIAM RIKER AND THIS IS MY CREW.

BENSLEY... I AM BENSLEY, A WORLD TRIBUNAL MEMBER, AND IT IS OUR PLEASURE TO HAVE YOU WITH US.

YOU HAVE A BEAUTIFUL PLACE HERE, BENSLEY...

...BOTH THE NATURAL ELEMENTS AND THE SENTIENT-MADE.

YOU ARE KIND, RIKER... BUT WE WOULD BE FOOLISH NOT TO CARE FOR OUR WORLD.

--OTHERWISE, IT MIGHT NOT BE SO BEARABLE.

PLEASE...THIS WAY THROUGH THE GARDEN.

IT *HAS* TO BE BEAUTIFUL HERE--

I AM DEANNA TROI, AND I AM CURIOUS AS TO WHY YOU SAY FALTOS *HAS* TO BE SO BREATH-TAKING?

QUITE SIMPLY, MADAME TROI, IF YOU MUST BE STUCK SOMEWHERE, IT MIGHT AS WELL BE A PLEASANT ENVIRONMENT, NO?

"STUCK"?!

WAIT, BENSLEY, SURELY YOUR PEOPLE ARE CAPABLE OF SPACE-FLIGHT.

AND, IF THEY'RE NOT-- THE FEDERATION, AS PART OF OUR PEACEFUL OVERTURES WITH YOUR WORLD--

--WOULD GLADLY PROVIDE INSTRUCTORS AND TECHNOLOGY FOR SUCH.

A MOST GRACIOUS OFFER... I WILL INFORM THE TRIBUNAL OF YOUR GENEROUS NATURE.

IF YOU WOULD LIKE, YOU MAY BRING THAT UP WITH THE OTHERS IN OUR CHAMBERS MOMENTARILY.

THIS WAY, WON'T YOU?

COMMANDER--?

I AM CONCERNED ABOUT SOME OF THE THINGS BENSLEY SAID.

MORE IMPORTANT -- I DO NOT *FEEL RIGHT* ABOUT THIS PLACE.

WITH ALL DUE RESPECT TO YOUR BETAZOID ANCESTRY AND TALENTS, DEANNA, I AM NOT QUITE SO WORRIED.

EVERYTHING HERE SEEMS RATHER COMFORTABLE AND EXTRAORDINARILY NICE.

VISITORS FROM THE ENTERPRISE, ENTER, PLEASE...

...AND BE RECEIVED BY FALTOS'S WORLD TRIBUNAL.

8

PLEASE...BE SEATED AND WE WILL BEGIN THIS DEBRIEFING.

I AM *BELE.* YOU'VE MET BENSLEY AND, TO HIS LEFT, IS *KRAW.*

WE TRUST YOU ARE--

--AND *WILL BE* COMFORTABLE.

WE ALREADY HAVE QUARTERS PREPARED FOR YOUR TEAM PRESENT...

...BUT WE WILL NEED TO KNOW HOW MANY, IN TOTAL, ARE ABOARD YOUR SHIP.

IT WILL NOT BE NECESSARY TO SUPPLY ACCOMMODATIONS FOR THE PASSENGERS AND CREW OF OUR SHIP, KRAW.

THEY ALREADY HAVE ADEQUATE ARRANGEMENTS ON THE SHIP ITSELF. BUT THANK YOU FOR THAT CONSIDERATION.

BELE, IT SHOULD BE KNOWN THAT THEY HAVE NOT BEEN TOLD YET.

THEN THEY DO NOT KNOW--

--THAT THEIR SHIP IS TO BE DISMANTLED?

STRANGE.

WHAT?!

NO!

WORF, WAIT--!

I *KNEW* THIS WORLD WAS NOT TO BE TRUSTED!

YOU WILL TAKE YOUR SEAT BEFORE THE TRIBUNAL, KLINGON! I WOULD LIKE TO THINK MY PEOPLE WOULD HAVE QUIETED DOWN BY NOW!

UNFORTUNATELY, YOU HAVE NO REAL CHOICE IN THIS MATTER--

--LIKE THE THOUSANDS WHO'VE ARRIVED AT FALTOS EVERY *CYCLE* BEFORE YOU--

-- YOU ARE TRAPPED HERE FOREVER!

THERE IS NO WAY OUT!

YOUR SHIP IS USELESS TO YOU HERE--

--FOR THERE IS NOWHERE TO GO!

9

ARE YOU SAYING YOU'RE *KEEPING* US HERE?

WERE WE *BROUGHT* HERE TO BE YOUR PRISONERS?

YOU WERE *NOT* BROUGHT HERE--YOU CAME OF YOUR OWN FREE WILL. WE ALL DID.

YOU *CROSSED* OVER INTO FALTOS'S PLANE OF EXISTENCE, SEARCHING FOR IT, OR SOMETHING LIKE IT-- AS I DID SIXTY-THREE STANDARD CYCLES AGO.

PEOPLE ALWAYS *TRY* TO GET AWAY... UNSUCCESSFULLY...AS DID I...

BUT, LIKE ALL THE OTHERS, I TOO GAVE UP AND JOINED THE HARMONIOUS LIFE FALTOS OFFERS.

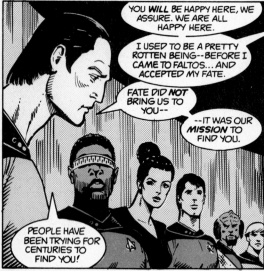

YOU *WILL* BE HAPPY HERE, WE ASSURE. WE ARE ALL HAPPY HERE.

I USED TO BE A PRETTY ROTTEN BEING--BEFORE I CAME TO FALTOS... AND ACCEPTED MY FATE.

FATE DID *NOT* BRING US TO YOU--

--IT WAS OUR *MISSION* TO FIND YOU.

PEOPLE HAVE BEEN TRYING FOR CENTURIES TO FIND YOU!

WELL, YOU FOUND IT...

...SO RELAX AND ENJOY IT.

NOW--WE CAN START TELEPORTING YOUR PEOPLE DOWN AS SOON AS--

NO! WE CANNOT SIMPLY *STAY* HERE!

IT IS OUR *NATURE* TO KEEP MOVING-- TO KEEP EXPLORING... LEARNING!

APPARENTLY NATURE HAS *OTHER* PLANS FOR YOU.

WE ARE SORRY. IT *IS* HARD TO ADJUST...

BUT YOU *WILL* ADJUST.

EVERYONE DOES.

COMMANDER, WE SHOULD HAVE SOME *TIME*.

YES. BENSLEY, THIS IS ALL SO MUCH TO CONSIDER...WE MUST CONSULT WITH OUR SUPERIORS.

VERY WELL.

BUT IT WILL BE BEST FOR YOU TO COME TO GRIPS WITH THIS SITUATION.

10

145

CAPTAIN, IT IS MY CONSIDERED OPINION THAT THIS SITUATION MIGHT BENEFIT FROM YOUR DIPLOMATIC EXPERTISE.

COUNSELOR, DO YOU THINK IT WISE FOR THE CAPTAIN TO--

SIR, FALTOS IS TOTALLY DEVOID OF MALICE ON EVERY LEVEL...

TO PARAPHRASE THE ANCIENT CLICHÉ-- IT IS ALMOST *TOO* SAFE.

IN THAT CASE, I WILL BE GLAD TO BEAM DOWN TO HELP, AND I SUSPECT THEIR TRIBUNAL *WOULD* AID *US* IF THEY--

EXCUSE ME, SIR, LAFORGE IS TRYING TO TELL ME SOMETHING.

UNDERSTOOD, COUNSELOR-- ANY AND ALL SUGGESTIONS ARE WELCOMED AT THIS POINT.

DEANNA...WE WERE JUST THINKING...IF DATA KNEW HOW TO GET *IN* TO FALTOS--

IT WOULD ONLY SEEM LOGICAL THAT SOMEWHERE INSIDE ME, I MUST HAVE THE INFORMATION NEEDED TO GET *OUT*.

WHOEVER LEFT THIS DATA IN ME--MAYBE EVEN DOCTOR SOONG HIMSELF--MIGHT HAVE BEEN SOMEONE WHO WAS ABLE TO ESCAPE FALTOS.

THOUGH THE TRIBUNAL SEEMS CERTAIN OF THE FACT THAT NO ONE'S BEEN ABLE TO GET OUT.

TO DIGRESS FOR A MOMENT--ANYONE BESIDES ME NOTICE THE SIMILARITIES BETWEEN BENSLEY AND THAT CRYSTAL-LINE "LIFE-LEECH" THAT DESTROYED THE EARTH-COLONY WHERE I WAS FIRST DISCOVERED?

DATA...THAT *WOULD* TIE IN WITH THIS ENTIRE CITY MADE OF CRYSTAL.

I DID FEEL SOMETHING FAMILIAR HERE RIGHT FROM THE START... DATA WOULD SEEM TO BE MAKING COMPUTERIZED FREE ASSOCIATIONS. AND ALONG THOSE SAME LINES:

THAT OTHER CREATURE WAS PURE EVIL-- CAN BENSLEY BE TRUSTED?

EVERYONE HERE SEEMS SO BENEVOLENT-- WOULD IT NOT BE POSSIBLE THAT SOMEONE OR THING WAS *BANISHED* FROM FALTOS?

SOUNDS TO ME LIKE YOU'RE HAVING TROUBLE GETTING DIRECTLY AT SOMETHING THAT THAT THING MIGHT'VE GOTTEN INSIDE YOU.

QUESTION IS-- HOW DO *WE* GET IT OUT?

12

WAIT--DID WE NOT RETRIEVE SOMETHING FROM INSIDE LIEUTENANT DATA ONCE BEFO--

EXACTLY WHAT I WAS THINKING, CAPTAIN...

THAT WAS THE TIME WE FACED THE CRYSTAL CREATURE.

CAPTAIN, ONCE AGAIN I MAY UNCONSCIOUSLY BE OUR ONLY HOPE.

VERY WELL...I WILL BE DOWN PRESENTLY WITH JUST THE TEAM FOR THIS DELICATE OPERATION.

PICARD OUT.

WE ARE PLEASED THAT YOUR COLLEAGUES HAVE ACQUIESCED AND WILL JOIN US SHORTLY.

THREE ARRIVALS IS NOT EXACTLY OPENING THE FLOOD-GATES, BELE.

WE MUST BREAK A STORY LIKE THIS TO OUR PEOPLE WITH THE UTMOST OF CARE, KRAW.

I UNDERSTAND. THE ENTERPRISE-- WHICH STILL SEEMS SOMEHOW DISTANTLY FAMILIAR TO ME-- IS QUITE LARGE, AND ITS NUMBERS DO CONSTITUTE THE LARGEST MIGRATION ONTO FALTOS, ACCORDING TO LEGENDS.

IF ONLY HALF YOUR PEOPLE REACT LIKE MY FOUR-MAN CREW AND I REACTED WHEN WE FIRST HIT THIS PLANET, THERE COULD BE *TROUBLE* ON FALTOS FOR THE FIRST TIME SINCE--

SINCE THE CREATOR ABANDONED FALTOS AT THE DAWN OF TIME.

YES...THAT IS WHAT I WAS GOING TO SAY, KRAW...YES.

13

147

GREETINGS, PEOPLE OF FALTOS... I AM CAPTAIN JEAN-LUC PICARD.

THIS IS MY SHIP'S DOCTOR, BEVERLY CRUSHER--

--AND CHIEF ENGINEER, LIEUTENANT ARGYLE.

WELCOME, CAPTAIN...I AM KRAW.

...AND THIS IS MY FELLOW COUNCILLOR, BELE.

I LOOK FORWARD TO MEETING YOUR ENTIRE TRIBUNAL SHORTLY, KRAW...

...BUT I MUST CONVENE WITH MY AWAY TEAM FIRST FOR A COMPLETE BRIEFING.

UNUSUAL, CAPTAIN...

BUT ANYTHING TO MAKE YOU AND YOUR PEOPLE COMFORTABLE HERE ON FALTOS.

THANK YOU, FALTOSIANS. WE WILL BE THERE.

WE WILL MEET IN OUR CHAMBERS IN THREE SEGMENTS.

THIS WAY, SIR.

YES. THIS PLANET IS RATHER TRANQUIL.

OBVIOUSLY THAT'S THE REACTION THIS PLACE BANKS ON, SIR.

IT DOES TAKE SOME OF THE FIGHT OUT OF YOU...

A LOT LIKE A RETIREMENT COMMUNITY, NO?

BUT FOR WHATEVER REASONS, WE'D BETTER AT LEAST TRY TO LIKE THIS PLACE.

UNLESS OUR PLANNED PROCEDURE ACTUALLY WORKS, TASHA.

CAPTAIN... DATA IS READY...

WE TRUST THE DOCTOR AND THE CHIEF ARE PREPARED AS WELL.

14

THIS ISN'T GOING TO HURT DATA, IS IT?

GEORDI... PLEASE--

--MY EMBARRASSMENT IS ALREADY OVERWHELMING.

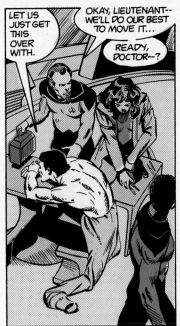

LET US JUST GET THIS OVER WITH.

OKAY, LIEUTENANT-- WE'LL DO OUR BEST TO MOVE IT...

READY, DOCTOR--?

I HATE DOING THIS, ARGYLE... OPERATING ON A SYNTHETIC MAN--

--ESPECIALLY WHEN I CAN'T PROMISE RESULTS.

HOW DO YOU THINK I FEEL?

WORKING ON A MAN, SYNTHETIC OR NOT, DOESN'T MAKE THIS ANY EASIER FOR ME.

DOCTOR...ONCE AGAIN, MAY I REQUEST THAT YOU DO YOUR BEST TO CONCEAL MY SECRET FROM THE OTHERS?

I FULLY UNDERSTAND, DATA-- NOBODY LIKES THEIR TURN-ONS AND TURN-OFFS TO BE COMMON KNOW-LEDGE.

MOST PEOPLE CONSIDER THAT PRIVATE INFORMATION.

I AM MORE CONCERNED ABOUT AMPLIFYING THE DIFFERENCES BETWEEN MYSELF AND THE REST OF YO--

THUNK

ALL RIGHT, DOCTOR... WHERE TO BEGIN?

IF I REMEMBER CORRECTLY...

15

THERE.

NO PROBLEM HERE WITH HUMANOID ECTODERMAL ENTRIES.

THIS IS WHERE I TAKE OVER.

WILL, I MUST CONFESS IT WAS VERY HARD FOR ME TO FOLLOW DATA'S ORDERS EARLIER. BUT SEEING HIM LIKE THIS I REALIZE HOW MUCH BIGGER THAN THE TWO OF US THIS ALL IS.

TELL ME, WILL... DO YOU ANTICIPATE ANY TROUBLE WITH THIS TRIBUNAL?

I SINCERELY DOUBT IT, CAPTAIN... THERE'S NEVER ANY REAL TROUBLE HERE APPARENTLY.

FRANKLY, IF ONE MUST BE STUCK SOMEWHERE, THIS *IS* THE PLACE TO BE STUCK.

SMALL CONSOLATION FOR THOSE OF US WHO ARE NOT READY TO STOP MOVING AND *BE* STUCK YET.

DOCTOR CRUSHER, I AM GOING TO HAVE TO BYPASS SEVERAL LAYERS OF DATA'S ACCESS CODES--

--BY ATTACHING AN AUXILIARY KEYBOARD TO MONITOR DATA'S INFORMATION BANKS.

16

COMPUTER: SHOW ME FILES A-001 THROUGH D-999.

I GOTTA START SOMEWHERE.

WAIT-- WHAT'S THIS ALREADY--?

LET ME JUST TRY SOMETHING HERE...

TAKA TAK TAK

DAMN!

NOTHING.

WELL, JUST BECAUSE THAT DIDN'T WORK DOESN'T MEAN--

HEY! HEY! LOOK AT THIS, BEVERLY!

I'M AFRAID ALL THOSE NUMBERS ARE NOTHING TO ME, CHIEF.

TAKA TAK

I'M SORRY, TOO. THIS IS ALL VERY FRUSTRATING TO ME... I SHOULD BE DOING MORE.

DOCTOR CRUSHER-- YOU HAVE DONE YOUR DUTY...

...AND WORKING SIDE BY SIDE WITH CHIEF ARGYLE, I SENSE THAT YOUR WORK IS ON THE VERGE OF--

THAT'S IT!

I'VE BROKEN DATA'S SOONG ACCESS CODE!

CLOSE 'IM UP, DOC.

JUST ONE MORE--! THERE.

WAY TO GO, DATA, YOU DID IT!

UHHHHH... IT, MY FRIEND, WAS DONE FOR ME.

IT...IT...WHAT EXACTLY IS IT?

WHAT DO WE HAVE NOW THAT WE DIDN'T HAVE MOMENTS AGO?

17

151

PLEASE... CAPTAIN... A MOMENT...

CHIEF ARGYLE, YOU DID *SAVE* THE ACCESS CODE FOR ME, DID YOU NOT? HAVING THE SOONG FILE WILL BE A BOON TO RESEARCH SCIENCE THE GALAXY OVER.

I BELIEVE THAT IT'S YOURS FOR THE ASKING, DATA, OLD BOY.

DATA, I REALIZE YOU HAVE JUST BEEN THROUGH A LOT, BUT, WE *MUST* KNOW--

--CAN YOU NOW GET THE ENTERPRISE OUT OF HERE?

CAPTAIN, I CAN NOW GET ANYONE AND ANYTHING OUT OF HERE.

JUST LIKE THE CRYSTAL-CREATURE SOONG WAS STUDYING GOT OUT OF HERE.

THE EQUATIONS FOR DOING SO ARE REALLY RATHER SIMPLISTIC.

WAIT A MINUTE, BELE AND KRAW MENTIONED SOMETHING ABOUT SOMEONE WHO GOT AWAY EARLIER.

HMMM COULD SOONG HAVE DELIBERATELY CON-FRONTED THAT ESCAPED FALTOSIAN TO GET THE SECRET OF THIS WORLD FROM IT?

AND HOW DO YOU GET A MALEVOLENT ENTITY LIKE THAT TO GIVE YOU ANY INFORMATION-- LET ALONE THE GREATEST SECRET IN THE UNIVERSE?

I CANNOT SAY FOR CERTAIN.

BUT I DO KNOW NOW THAT SOONG'S RESEARCH OF THAT CRYSTALLINE ENERGY-BEING *IS* WHAT LED IT DIRECTLY TO SOONG'S LAB COLONY.

WHICH ULTIMATELY LED ALL HIS ASSISTANTS AND COLONISTS TO THEIR DEATHS AT THAT CREATURE'S HAND.

IT IS LIKE FINDING OUT ONE'S OWN FATHER WAS KHAN NOONIEN SINGH HIMSELF.

ALL THOSE DEAD BY SOONG'S DEEDS...

AND ALL THEIR THOUGHTS AND KNOWLEDGE *HIDDEN* WITHIN ME FOR POSTERITY.

I CANNOT TELL WHETHER SOONG KNEW WHAT WOULD HAPPEN-- OR IF HE TOO WAS A PATHETIC VICTIM OF A GREAT ACCIDENT OF FATE OR IF, IN FACT, HE WAS THE VICTIM OF HIS OWN QUEST FOR ADVANCED KNOWLEDGE.

18

I'M AFRAID ALL OF YOUR QUESTIONS WILL HAVE TO WAIT, LIEUTENANT. PICARD TO ENTERPRISE.

ENTERPRISE, SIR.

LOCK COORDINATES AND BEAM ARGYLE, CRUSHER, LAFORGE AND DATA BACK ABOARD THE SHIP.

THEY'LL BE PREPARING THE ENTERPRISE FOR DEPARTURE MANEUVERS. PICARD OUT.

THE REST OF YOU--TO THE TRIBUNAL'S CHAMBERS WITH ME. RIKER, LEAD THE WAY.

NOBODY'S HERE.

IT WOULD APPEAR WE ARE A BIT EARLY FOR OUR MEETING, CAPTAIN.

GOOD. THAT WILL GIVE THE OTHERS SOME TIME TO WORK BACK ON THE SHIP.

I DO NOT SENSE THAT THERE IS MUCH TIME, THOUGH, CAPTAIN. I--

WE ARE PLEASED THAT YOU HAVE COME TO ACCEPT YOUR FUTURE HERE SO SOON.

CAPTAIN PICARD, IS IT?

CAPTAIN-- THEY'RE HERE--!

GREETINGS, WORLD TRIBUNAL, I AM JEAN-LUC PICARD, CAPTAIN OF THE ENTERPRISE.

AND I AM BELE.

AND WE VOW THAT YOU AND YOUR NUMEROUS PEOPLES WILL HAVE A LIFETIME OF CONTENTMENT HERE ON FALTOS, CAPTAIN.

I AM SORRY, BELE--

--TEMPTING THOUGH YOUR WORDS MAKE IT SOUND...

WE WILL BE LEAVING FALTOS.

19

LEAVING, CAPTAIN PICARD? OH, PLEASE...HARDLY.

REALLY...YOU ARE ONLY PUTTING OFF THE INEVITABLE, SIR.

NOBODY LEAVES FALTOS.

NO...WE HAVE A WAY TO VACATE YOUR WORLD... AND WE INTEND TO DO JUST THAT.
ONE OF MY CREW WAS APPARENTLY CREATED BY A MAN IN TOUCH WITH THE ONE WHO ESCAPED YOUR WORLD.

WE HAVE THE KNOWLEDGE... AND WE'RE USING IT.

THE ONE WHO ESCAPED--?

THE CREATOR--?

AND WE ARE HERE BEFORE YOU TO EXTEND OUR HAND--

--TO HELP ANY OF YOU OR YOUR PEOPLE TO GET AWAY FROM FALTOS... IF THEY SO WISH.

RETURN TO MY SHATTERED WORLD...

...HAVE NO OTHERS OF MY RACE...NO ONE TO LOVE...

I QUITE AGREE.

FALTOS WAS CREATED FOR THE LUCKY FEW WHO HAPPENED UPON IT.

IT IS A PLACE FOR THE PRIVILEGED.

NO, I WAS MEANT TO BE HERE.

AT LEAST LET US THEN EXTEND THIS OFFER TO YOUR PEOPLE...

SURELY THOSE WHO ARE NOT PRESENT HERE TODAY MUST REALIZE THIS IS THEIR CHANCE FOR FREEDOM.

NO.

WE MUST KEEP THIS FROM OUR PEOPLE.

WE HAVE BEEN ELECTED TO HELP KEEP THE PEACE...

AND IT IS OUR CONSIDERED OPINION THAT BY OFFERING OPTIONS, THE PEACE MIGHT BE UPSET.

20

BUT SURELY THERE ARE SOME WHO WOULD LIKE TO GO...

WE HAVE MADE OUR DECISION.

IF YOU ARE LEAVING, YOU SHOULD DO SO QUICKLY.

BEFORE YOUR NEWS OF OFFERS *TAINTS* THE TRANQUILLITY OF FALTOS.

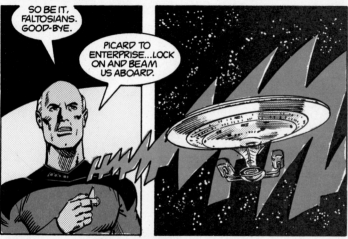

SO BE IT, FALTOSIANS. GOOD-BYE.

PICARD TO ENTERPRISE...LOCK ON AND BEAM US ABOARD.

DATA...JOINING BOTH TRANSPORTER AND WARP TECHNOLOGY LIKE THIS IS MOST UNORTHODOX.

ARE YOU QUITE CERTAIN THIS WILL GET US OUT OF HERE SAFELY?

SAFELY? I CANNOT BE CERTAIN OF OUR SAFETY, SIR...

BUT WE *WILL* GET OUT OF HERE.

WARP FACTOR 9.3, CHIEF ARGYLE.

BUT, DATA, THAT'S SO *EXTREME.* ARE YOU--

YES. I AM SUUUUURRREEEE.

THEY HAVE OUR KNOWLEDGE... AND THEY WILL TELL ALL.

AND DURING THE NEXT CONVERGENCE, FALTOS WILL BE UNDONE.

I CANNOT LET THAT BE.

21

DATA, WE ARE SHAKING APART!

ARGYLE...FULL REVERSE.

BUT LIEUTENANT--

FULL REVERSE.

IF YOU WILL GO--

--YOU WILL NOT TAKE ALL WE HAVE.

AARRGGH!

DATA, ARE YOU--

MY HEAD... MY HEAD...

HEY! DATA... WE'VE DONE IT! WE'RE BACK IN SECTOR 902!

UHHH... I TOLD YOU...I COULD...

EASY, DATA...CROSSING THE PLANES HAS DRAINED YOU. DUPLICATE SOONG'S FILE IN THE SHIP'S COMPUTER AND TAKE SOME TIME TO RECUPERATE.

IT WAS NOT THE CROSSING THAT DRAINED ME...

...THOUGH DRAINED IS WHAT I LITERALLY AM.

I COULD FEEL BENSLEY INSIDE MY HEAD... HE HAS SOMEHOW TAKEN THE FILE FROM ME. UNLIKE THE ENERGY-LEECH WE'D MET BEFORE...

BENSLEY USED HIS ABILITY TO RETRIEVE KNOWLEDGE FROM MY BRAIN-- RATHER THAN SUCK THE ENTIRE LIFE FROM MY BODY. HE WAS PROTECTING HIS WORLD-- AND NOW, UNFORTUNATELY, FALTOS IS LOST TO US FOREVER.

CAPTAIN'S LOG; STARDATE 41758.1:

IN A WAY, IT IS FITTING THAT THE IMPERFECTIONS OF HUMANITY WILL STILL BE UNABLE TO REACH THE PARADISE OF FALTOS...SINCE WE REMAIN UNABLE TO CHART ITS PRECISE WHEREABOUTS.

THE FEDERATION WILL HAVE TO BE CONTENT WITH THE KNOWLEDGE THAT THEY NOW HAVE A SHIP-LOAD OF PEOPLE WHO'VE BEEN TO FALTOS AND BACK...

AND WHO WERE NOW ABLE TO CONTRIBUTE TO FALTOS'S ALREADY FAULTLESS LEGEND.

THE END

C O V E R S

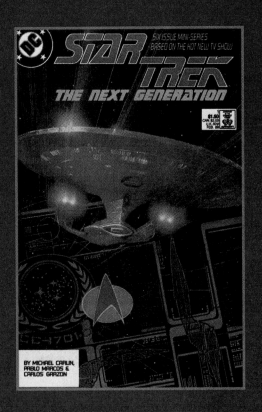

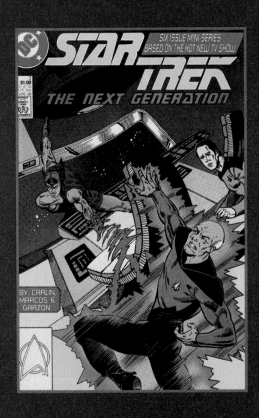

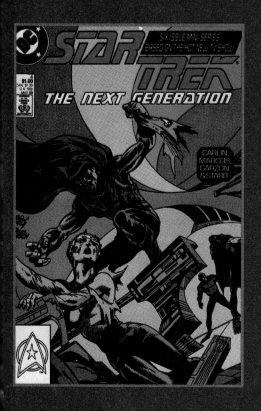

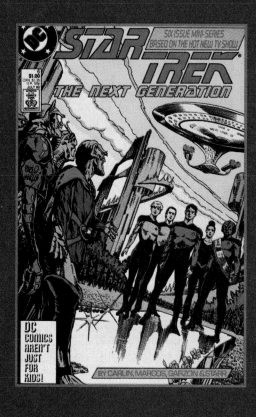

You CAN FIND MORE STAR-SPANNING ADVENTURES IN THE FOLLOWING BOOKS FROM TITAN:

STAR TREK: DEBT OF HONOR
CHRIS CLAREMONT/ADAM HUGHES/
KARL STORY

STAR TREK: TESTS OF COURAGE
HOWARD WEINSTEIN/ROD WHIGHAM/
GORDON PURCELL/ARNE STARR/
CARLOS GARZON

STAR TREK: WHO KILLED CAPTAIN KIRK?
PETER DAVID/TOM SUTTON/
GORDON PURCELL/RICARDO VILLAGRAN

STAR TREK: THE NEXT GENERATION—THE STAR LOST
MICHAEL JAN FRIEDMAN/
PETER KRAUSE/PABLO MARCOS

STAR TREK: THE ASHES OF EDEN
WILLIAM SHATNER WITH
JUDITH & GARFIELD REEVES-STEVENS/
STEVE ERWIN/JIMMY PALMIOTTI